Experiencing Music Composition in Grades K–2

Experiencing Music Composition in Grades K–2

Michele Kaschub and Janice P. Smith

Published in partnership with
National Association for Music Education

ROWMAN & LITTLEFIELD
Lanham • Boulder • New York • London

Published in partnership with National Association for Music Education

Published by Rowman & Littlefield
An imprint of The Rowman & Littlefield Publishing Group, Inc.
4501 Forbes Boulevard, Suite 200, Lanham, Maryland 20706
www.rowman.com

86-90 Paul Street, London EC2A 4NE

Copyright © 2022 by Michele Kaschub and Janice P. Smith

All rights reserved. No part of this book may be reproduced in any form or by any electronic or mechanical means, including information storage and retrieval systems, without written permission from the publisher, except by a reviewer who may quote passages in a review.

British Library Cataloguing in Publication Information Available

Library of Congress Cataloging-in-Publication Data

Names: Kaschub, Michele, 1967- author. | Smith, Janice P., author. | National Association for Music Education.
Title: Experiencing music composition in grades K–2 / Michele Kaschub and Janice P. Smith.
Description: Lanham : Rowman & Littlefield Publishers, 2022. | "Published in partnership with National Association for Music Education" | Includes bibliographical references and index. | Summary: "Experiencing Music Composition Grades K-2 features pedagogical strategies and practical advice for teachers coupled with fifteen engaging lessons tailored to meet the needs and interests of very young musicians"— Provided by publisher.
Identifiers: LCCN 2022023332 (print) | LCCN 2022023333 (ebook) | ISBN 9781475867893 (cloth) | ISBN 9781475867909 (paperback) | ISBN 9781475867916 (ebook)
Subjects: LCSH: Composition (Music)—Instruction and study | Music—Instruction and study—Outlines, syllabi, etc. | Education, Primary—Activity programs.
Classification: LCC MT40 .K276 2022 (print) | LCC MT40 (ebook) | DDC 372.87/4—dc23/eng/20220517
LC record available at https://lccn.loc.gov/2022023332
LC ebook record available at https://lccn.loc.gov/2022023333

Contents

About the Companion Website	vii
Introduction	ix

SECTION 1: TEACHING AND LEARNING WITH *EXPERIENCING MUSIC COMPOSITION*   1

1   The *Experiencing Music Composition* Program   3
     Experiencing Music Composition and the National Arts Standards for Music   4
     Teaching Music Composition with the *National Arts Standards* for *Music*   4

2   What to Expect from Very Young Composers   9
     Typical Characteristics of Composers in Grades K–2   9
     Needs of Very Young Composers   9
     Typical Qualities of Works by Composers in Grades K–2   10

3   How to Use This Book   11

SECTION 2: FACILITATING THE WORK OF VERY YOUNG COMPOSERS   13

4   Compositional Capacities   15
     On Composing   15
        Feelingful Intention   15
        Developing the Capacity of Feelingful Intention   16
        Musical Expressivity   16
        More about the M.U.S.T.S.   16
        Developing the Capacity of Musical Expressivity   19
        Artistic Craftsmanship   20
        Techniques and Etudes for Grades K–2   20
        Developing the Capacity of Artistic Craftsmanship   25
     Final Thoughts   25

5   Using *Sketchpages*   27
     Guiding the Journey   27
     Introducing *Sketchpages* to very Young Composers   27
     Sketchpages as Multitaskers   28

SECTION 3: CREATIVE POSITIVE COMPOSITIONAL EXPERIENCES   31

6   Composition Requires a Different Kind of Teaching   33
     Working with "In-process" Composers   36
     Anchoring Knowledge, Inviting Inspiration   37

| | Guidelines for Sharing Compositions—Giving and Receiving Feedback | 39 |
| | Making the Most of Limited Timeframes | 43 |

SECTION 4: TEACHER GUIDES AND STUDENT *SKETCHPAGES*   45

7	Teacher Guides and Student *Sketchpages*	47
	Curricular Organization	47

Projects for Kindergarten   49

8	*Songwriting*—Teddy Bear Lullabies	51
9	*Composing and Visual Media*—Sonifying Characters: The Gingerbread Man	55
10	*Instrumental Music*—Stormy Weather	63
11	*Electronic Music and Digital Media*—Achieving Artistry with Apps	67
12	*Music Theater*—Birthday Wishes	71

Projects for Grade 1   75

13	*Songwriting*—Field Trip Song	77
14	*Composition and Visual Media*—Background Music for Storytelling	81
15	*Instrumental Music*—Duets with Two Sounds: A Musical Conversation	85
16	*Electronic Music and Digital Media*—Sound Blocks and Patterns	89
17	*Music Theater*—Making a "When I Grow Up, I Want to Be" Song	93

Projects for Grade 2   99

18	*Songwriting*—A Song for Grandparents' Day	101
19	*Composition and Visual Media*—Exploring Leitmotif: The Mitten	105
20	*Instrumental Music*—Chamber Music Trios	109
21	*Electronic Music and Digital Media*—Terrific Textures	115
22	*Music Theater*—Incidental Music for Puppet Theater	119

Appendix: Notation Templates	125
Index	131
About the Authors	135

About the Companion Website

https://rowman.com/ISBN/9781475867893/Experiencing-Music-Composition-in-Grades-K%E2%80%932

We have created a website to accompany *Experiencing Music Composition: Grades K–2*. Full-color versions of each *Sketchpage* are provided so that teachers may project these images when facilitating classroom instruction or guiding whole class composition activities. Black and white versions of each *Sketchpage* are provided so that teachers may print and distribute them to students.

Introduction

Welcome to Experiencing Music Composition!

Composing music is a wonderful experience for children. It allows them to discover their musical imaginations as they create songs and pieces to suit their needs and interests and which they can share with others. Often people think that children need extensive formal training in music theory or considerable skill as performers to compose, but we have found that just about everyone can create music with a little help and some useful strategies. This book offers exactly that. It provides guidance for teachers who are ready to nurture creative spirits and suggests tools young composers can use to capture and manage their many musical ideas.

You do not have to be a professional composer to guide children as they create their own music, but some formal music training can be helpful. Active listening skills, a willingness to explore and consider a broad range of musical possibilities, some practice at asking critical questions of young composers about their work, and a strong belief that music will emerge from what may appear to be a busy, messy, and sometimes rather loud sound environment are all you need. These skills and dispositions combined with a focused approach will allow you and your students to find musical satisfaction and ongoing success.

In the following sections we will introduce the *Experiencing Music Composition* approach and present a snapshot of young composers and their work across Grades K–2. The teaching and learning tools of *Experiencing Music Composition* can be used by composers of all ages to develop capacities critical in creating original music. These three capacities—*feelingful intention*, *musical expressivity*, and *artistic craftsmanship*—provide the springboard that advances children's work from collections of random sounds and brief musical gestures to thoughtfully created, expressive pieces. The *Sketchpages* are graphic organizers that guide students and their teachers in thinking through their compositional ideas. They are included with every lesson to support the development of musical artistry. Each lesson also includes suggestions for productive sharing and feedback in a variety of formats to help composers assess their progress and evaluate the quality of their work.

We are excited that you and your young musicians are embarking on an exciting journey in creating original music and we hope that you will love *Experiencing Music Composition!*

Section 1

TEACHING AND LEARNING WITH
EXPERIENCING MUSIC COMPOSITION

Chapter 1

The *Experiencing Music Composition* Program

Experiencing Music Composition is focused on providing opportunities for K–12 students to create original music through composition. The approach progresses from teacher-facilitated collaborative work, through partnered and small group activities, toward projects where the students assume complete artistic autonomy. The lessons and activities of the program are designed to challenge students' skills and understandings as they explore the expressive potentials of sound across different genres, settings, and media.

The *Experiencing Music Composition* program is suitable for use in private teaching studios, school music programs, and any other place where young people make music. The compositional tasks of the program parallel those undertaken by singer-songwriters, movie score composers, video game score composers, commercial jingles creators, and everything in between. Students create songs, instrumental ensembles, pieces partnered with electronic media, music to accompany art installations, film, music theater and much, much more.

Graphic organizers, called *Sketchpages*, guide and enhance this work. Designed specifically to promote student creativity and develop key compositional skills, *Sketchpages* are a mix of doodle space and composer's notebook. As students work with these pages, they are invited to imagine how their music might sound and how others may experience those sounds as performers and listeners. Students quickly learn to identify and develop the feelings, thoughts, and ideas they wish to explore and share through their work. Further, they learn to use the tools and techniques of composition expressively to achieve artistic ends.

The *Experiencing Music Composition* promotes individuality. Students are encouraged to create music in a manner that reveals their unique musical ideas. This signature sound is often referred to as the composer's "voice." Just as many musical listeners easily recognize works of Aaron Copland, Ludwig van Beethoven, James Taylor, or Taylor Swift, so will members of your musical community be able to identify pieces that "belong" to a specific composer or group of collaborative composers. The emergence of "voice" is important because it reveals a clarity of music thought and the capacity to engage meaningfully with music over time.

While individual voice is an important development for any artist, isolation rarely leads to meaningful growth. The *Experiencing Music Composition* program emphasizes collaborative learning, facilitated sharing, and productive feedback through Composer's Circles—a forum in which composers may share their work and ask other members of the community for reactions, advice and suggestions. As composers interact with peers, teachers, performers, and others from the musical community-at-large, they are exposed to a broad palette of compositional tools, techniques and ideas that may shape or influence not only their current project but future projects as well. This social format provides an important counterpart to work that may be isolating and helps composers balance subjective and objective evaluations of their own work.

EXPERIENCING MUSIC COMPOSITION AND THE NATIONAL ARTS STANDARDS FOR MUSIC

The lessons and activities of the *Experiencing Music Composition* program can work seamlessly with the *National Arts Standards for Music*[1] addressing Creativity in K–8. Each lesson touches upon the Enduring Understandings and Essential Questions outlined within the standards while leaving the specific path to learning open. This kind of music learning is personally relevant and driven by each student's curiosities and passions for music. The compositional challenges that students face are authentic and true to the experience of composition in the world at large.

More specifically, composition allows students to explore their creative ideas, concepts and feeling through the creation of music that represents their unique artistic perspectives. Drawing on a variety of sources and influences, composers engage with perceptual and conceptual knowledge to imagine music for a variety of purposes. Composers use their previous experiences and emerging expertise to develop expressive intent. As they set feelingful intentions and engage in artistic craftsmanship, they enter an exciting process of testing, evaluating, selecting, and refining their musical ideas. When the work is finished, composers may decide to present it to others.

However, not all compositions will be shared with an audience. For some composers and some composition activities, performance is not the goal. Some composers write only for themselves. Even with encouragement from others to share what they have created, they may choose not to do so. This choice represents a process of selection, analysis, and evaluation in which the student has decided not to make a particular work public. If and when composers choose to share their music, either by performing it themselves or through the performance of others, they will need to select, analyze, interpret, rehearse, evaluate, refine, and present their creations in the role of performer or as the adviser to the performers.

Composers are often influenced by what they hear in the music of other composers. Moreover, as they listen to the work of others, composers select, analyze, interpret, and evaluate what they hear. They respond to selected influences by analyzing them and by using those influences in their own works. This is especially true of young composers who are learning to craft feelingful sounds. "I want to compose something like that" is a common reaction to music that has made a feelingful impact on them.

Finally, composition provides a way for students to connect their personal interests, experiences, and ideas to musical sounds. In doing so, they deepen their understanding of all aspects of creating, performing, and responding because all three actions must be considered by the composer. The ability to synthesize and relate experience and sound can be developed in students. The *National Standards for Music* provide curricular guidelines for this work. The *Experiencing Music Composition* approach, with its emphasis on the development of feelingful intention, musical expressivity, and artistic craftsmanship, offers teacher strategies for welcoming composition into their classrooms.

TEACHING MUSIC COMPOSITION WITH THE *NATIONAL ARTS STANDARDS* FOR *MUSIC*

In compositional work, the artistic process and learning must belong to the student. If teachers can predict that everyone will learn the same technique or have the same experience, then they are engaging students with etudes. Etudes are a particular type of compositional activity in which the teacher controls the artistic process for the express purpose of introducing students to a new technique or musical practice (for etude examples see pages 20–25). These activities are of value because they present specific aspects of artistic craftsmanship and music theory. However, they should not be confused with composing music.

Composition is an emergent process where students' artistic autonomy is critical. As students compose, they must be able to make musical and artistic choices that are meaningful within their understanding of music. The composition activities outlined in this book provide teachers with an opportunity to gently guide—rather than predict—product outcomes. The process and the resulting products must be student-centered and student-driven. Consequently, students may meet different standards at different times.

While the standards provide guidelines, individual expressivity and voice are the goals of composing. The EMC approach provides teachers with the opportunity to truly tailor instruction to the needs of individual students. However, emergent learning can be a challenge to document. To help teachers manage this process, we suggest creating a standards checklist for each student. One possible example of this is shown in figures 1.1–1.3. This type of formative assessment can then inform future instruction.

Student Name _____

In the boxes, note the date and in which project or lesson you notice the student exhibiting these behaviors.

Standards	Emerging	Approaches	Meets	Exceeds
MU:Cr1.1.Ka With guidance, explore and experience music concepts (such as beat and melodic contour).				
MU:Cr1.1.Kb With guidance, generate musical ideas (such as movements or motives).				
MU:Cr2.1.Ka With guidance, demonstrate and choose favorite musical ideas.				
MU:Cr2.1.Kb With guidance, organize personal musical ideas using iconic notation and/or recording technology.				
MU:Cr3.1.Ka With guidance, apply personal, peer, and teacher feedback in refining personal musical ideas.				
MU:Cr3.1.Kb With guidance, apply personal, peer, and teacher feedback in refining personal musical ideas.				
MU:Cr3.2.Kc With guidance, demonstrate a final version of personal musical ideas to peers.				

Figure 1.1 National Arts Standards for Music, Creating, Grade K. *Source*: Adapted by Michele Kaschub & Janice Smith from the 2014 National Core Arts Standards, State Education Agency Directors of Arts Education.

Student Name _____

In the boxes, note the date and in which project or lesson you notice the student exhibiting these behaviors.

Standards	Emerging	Approaches	Meets	Exceeds
MU:Cr1.1.1a With limited guidance, create musical ideas (such as answering a musical question) for a specific purpose.				
MU:Cr1.1b With limited guidance, generate musical ideas in multiple tonalities (such as major and minor) and meters (such as duple and triple).				
MU:Cr2.1.1a With limited guidance, demonstrate and discuss personal reasons for selecting musical ideas that represent expressive intent.				
MU:Cr2.1.1b With limited guidance, use iconic or standard notation and/or recording technology to document and organize personal musical ideas.				
MU:Cr3.1.1a With limited guidance, discuss and apply personal, peer, and teacher feedback to refine personal musical ideas.				
MU:Cr3.2.1a With limited guidance, convey expressive intent for a specific purpose by presenting a final version of personal musical ideas to peers or informal audience.				

Figure 1.2 National Arts Standards for Music, Creating, Grade 1. *Source*: Adapted by Michele Kaschub & Janice Smith from the 2014 National Core Arts Standards, State Education Agency Directors of Arts Education.

Student Name _____

In the boxes, note the date and in which project or lesson you notice the student exhibiting these behaviors.

Standards	Emerging	Approaches	Meets	Exceeds
MU:Cr1.1.2a Improvise rhythmic and melodic patterns and musical ideas for a specific purpose.				
MU:Cr1.1.2b Generate musical patterns and ideas within the context of a given tonality (such as major and minor) and meter (such as duple and triple).				
MU:Cr2.1.2a Demonstrate and explain personal reasons for selecting patterns and ideas for music that represent expressive intent.				
MU:Cr2.1.2b Use iconic or standard notation and/or recording technology to combine, sequence, and document personal musical ideas.				
MU:Cr3.1.2a Interpret and apply personal, peer, and teacher feedback to revise personal music.				
MU:Cr3.2.2a Convey expressive intent or a specific purpose by presenting a final version of personal musical ideas to peers or informal audience.				

Figure 1.3 National Arts Standards for Music, Creating, Grade 2. *Source*: Adapted by Michele Kaschub & Janice Smith from the 2014 National Core Arts Standards, State Education Agency Directors of Arts Education.

NOTE

1. The 2014 *National Core Arts Standards* are available from State Education Agency Directors of Arts Education (SEADAE) at https://www.nationalartsstandards.org.

Chapter 2

What to Expect from Very Young Composers

The music that young composers create springs from their lived experiences and their imaginations. They are drawn to both the familiar and the novel and they enjoy borrowing musical material and folding it into their work. In many ways these attributes make them like all composers throughout history, but composers in grades K–2 also have attributes specific to their level of development. The following descriptions of young composers and their music may help you determine what is appropriate and useful in guiding the work of young composers.

TYPICAL CHARACTERISTICS OF COMPOSERS IN GRADES K–2

- Very young composers spontaneously create music as they play.
- Very young composers naturally explore how things make sounds and enjoy playing with sound sources.
- Very young composers are aware of how music is used in various places in their cultures.
- Very young composers vary widely in their musical backgrounds and experiences.
- Very young composers can begin to think about how they react to music.
- Very young composers can move from spontaneously created music to deliberate creation of music.
- Very young composers can begin to imagine how something feels and how sound can affect feeling.

NEEDS OF VERY YOUNG COMPOSERS

Very young composers need the opportunity to develop a repertoire of sounds which they can manipulate. They need the time, space, and materials to explore as they play. There needs to be free play with sound in order to understand what the sounds can express, even at an intuitive level. While they need to build a repertoire of familiar sounds, they also need to have experiences with high-quality musical sounds from a variety of cultures. Cheap, imitation instruments can lead to a false sense of what musical sounds can be. Educating children's ears should use the best quality, yet durable, sounds. For example, there is a vast difference in timbre between inexpensive finger cymbals and more resonant ones.

Related to the quality of sound is the opportunity to experiment with those sounds at a variety of dynamic levels. Very young children need opportunities to explore the full range of dynamics with many sound sources. Always playing the instruments quietly—or loudly—does not allow the children to acquire a sense of the expressive potential of the sounds. At these early stages it is about the process of sound exploration and pleasure in sounds for their own sake. During free play the children will often create their own patterns and structures and get caught up in the flow of using them as an adjunct to play.

While ideally this occurs as part of free play, it can also occur when the teacher brings an unfamiliar instrument to class and allows each child a turn at producing a sound on it (brass tree chime? tabla? accordion?) while encouraging them to think of new ways of producing the sounds. Teacher-guided products can occur once some exploration has taken place. The goal is to move very young composers from

"What does this do?"
To
"What can I do with this?"

TYPICAL QUALITIES OF WORKS BY COMPOSERS IN GRADES K–2

- Compositions connect to life in concrete ways. Their music is often about things that happen during the day.
- Compositions can be "fortuitous accidents" where pieces arise in the course of the day.
- Compositions prominently feature repetition.
- Compositions may quote familiar songs, but the lyrics and melodies may be added to or changed.
- Compositions may be inspired by games, toys, pictures, books.
- Compositions are often "storied" and are organized chronologically. Because children develop at different rates and maintain different sources of inspiration and intention, the shift from *"storied"* to *"expressive of"* pieces varies from child to child. Very young composers who are moving beyond sounds-based direct experiences may begin to:
  - develop an awareness of feelingful responses to music
  - consider a range of compositional intentions
  - intentionally experiment with different sounds and approaches to create a specific impact.
- Compositions tend to avoid the use of tension.
- Compositions favor predictability.

Chapter 3

How to Use This Book

Section 1 Compositional Capacities	Section 2 Using *Sketchpages*
Section 3 Creating Positive Compositional Experiences	Section 4 Teacher Guides and Student *Sketchpages*

This book is divided into four sections. Each section offers insights and tools for working with young composers. Sections 1–3 are designed to prepare educators to teach composition. Section 4 provides suggestions for implementing specific lessons. Section 1 introduces the key focus on the Experiencing Music Composition approach—the three compositional capacities that are the foundation of the composer's work. Numerous examples and resources are provided to prepare teachers to guide students as they develop specific skills and abilities related to each compositional capacity.

Section 2 focuses on the use of *Sketchpages*. These graphic organizers serve as creative spaces for teachers and students to use when planning compositions, actively composing, or reflecting on their work. *Sketchpages* can be used to organize group work or to help individual composers as they consider the music they wish to create. *Sketchpages* can also be useful data collection tools because they reveal the connections that students make between the three compositional capacities.

The music that young composers create represents a deeply personal investment. Sharing music with others places young composers in a vulnerable position. Section 3 offers guidance and strategies for sharing work, providing feedback, and encouraging future growth in a manner that fosters a positive learning environment and honors each composer's musical autonomy.

Section 4 contains teacher guides with ready-to-use *Sketchpages* to get you and your young composers creating original music in five different compositional genres. Each guide outlines one or more possible approaches to the lesson. They are intended to help you get started and to serve as models.

Section 2

FACILITATING THE WORK OF VERY YOUNG COMPOSERS

Chapter 4

Compositional Capacities

ON COMPOSING

All students have the ability to create music that is uniquely their own. The act of composing transcends the limits of verbal and mathematical representations and allows children to explore sound as a means of sharing who they are, what they think, and what they feel about their experiences in the world. It invites them to draw on the full breadth of their musical skills and understanding to create music that represents their unique insights. As such, composition is more than just an activity of music education; it is a process that draws together intellect and intuition, thinking and feeling, and the practical, and the inspired. It brings into reality thoughts and feelings that have only existed in the imagination and contributes to the creation of our individual and collective human spirit. Very young children seem to do this intuitively.

Just as some students find learning words easier than others—or read with greater comprehension or solve math problems more quickly—some children will have a more developed sense of music composition. Students' abilities not only depend on natural aptitude but also on the opportunities and the instruction they have had. Throughout *Experiencing Music Composition*, activities will focus on the development of three compositional capacities: feelingful intention, musical expressivity, and artistic craftsmanship. Each plays an integral role in the way we experience and understand music.

Feelingful Intention

Many times, very young children create musical motifs or short, repetitive pieces completely by chance. Teachers who recognize these "fortuitous accidents" as fledgling compositions can encourage very young composers to create more of them. As children develop music beyond these initial ideas, they can be guided to think about how their music makes them feel and how it might make others feel. The ability to consider the emotional impact of musical sounds is the capacity of *feelingful intention*.

Children know that music has the ability to communicate because they have encountered music that has aroused feelings in them. Simply suggesting to a child that she can create some music that conveys the impression of a familiar feeling can lead to a composition that is more expressive than one rooted in music notation.

For example, a group of children is very excited about a new classroom pet, in this case, a bunny. The teacher listens to their excited chatter and recognizes an opportunity to compose. She suggests that the students create music about what they feel as they take care of Mr. Fuzzy. Some of the students suggest a different perspective, that of how they feel as they watch him move around the classroom during play times. Still others want to create a piece about how the bunny feels when they all have gone home. Instruments are selected and the sounds of musical thinking soon fill the room. (This can also be done as a whole class activity for less experienced composers. Then agreement would be needed on the kind of music to be created.) The teacher hears rhythmic ostinatos, rising and falling melodies, and a few simple harmonies emerging from various spots around the room. When the students share their pieces, the teacher asks questions that help them identify how they have crafted their music. The names for these techniques can then be introduced and added to an ongoing list of compositional strategies that any composer may use to invite particular feelingful responses.

Developing the Capacity of Feelingful Intention

The intention to create music that sounds like feelings feel is implicit in all music. It is the *why* of music composition and the gateway to using compositional tools and techniques with artistic purpose. Very young musicians are aware of the feelingful impact of the music that they encounter, but their awareness may be more tacit than explicit. Below are some activities that may be used to help students develop the capacity of feelingful intention.

1. Ask the students to describe the feeling they get when they listen to a particular piece of music. Follow up with "What about the music makes you feel that way?" Be sure to share with the students that well-crafted music can invite different responses, so there may be many different answers.
2. Build chart of words that can be used to describe moods, feelings, and impressions. A sample is shown in figure 4.1, but students will have greater ownership in a resource that they create and will reference it more frequently than they will a teacher handout or pre-made poster.
3. Encourage students to experiment with different feelingful intentions when they perform. If a single phrase is played with opposite intentions, does the music and their feeling about it change? In what way?
4. Encourage students to identify the feelingful intention or intentions in their own work as well as in the work of their peers. Feelingful intentions may be outlined in the planning stages of the compositional process, but may also emerge organically as students explore and test their many musical ideas as a piece unfolds.
5. Building an awareness of feelingful intention and its role in shaping musical decision-making is a key component in the artistic development of very young composers.

Musical Expressivity

Music's expressive power relies on our ability to perceive the continually shifting balances within and between motion and stasis, unity and variety, sound and silence, tension and release, and stability and instability. These five musical principles, which we term "M.U.S.T.S.," correspond directly to the way we perceive changes in our condition and environment through the complex array of our internal and external senses. When children understand this connection, they learn to reference their own intuitive understandings and can draw on a personal bank of feelings that have arisen in their own experiences to consider how sound might be shaped to invite similar feelings. This skill allows composers to strategically select and shape how feelings are *sonified*—expressed in sound.

Continuing with our bunny example, some very young composers might recall the peaceful, gentle feeling of patting the bunny, but then the surprise when he jumps out of their laps (stability/instability). Some composers might try to organize sounds that parallel the feeling of anticipation (tension) that they felt when it would be their turn to care for the bunny. Other composers might sonify the feeling of excitement brought about by letting the bunny out of his hutch and watching him hop around the room. While each composer may pursue a different feelingful intention or focus on a different aspect of the experience, musical expressivity can be achieved if students are encouraged to use sounds in a balance that "feels right." In a whole class setting the teacher can encourage students to consider different options and how they might best be sonified.

More about the M.U.S.T.S.

The five principle pairs that comprise the M.U.S.T.S. can be found in our experience of a wide variety of music. While one or more of the principle pairs may be more prominent than others in a given work or section of a piece, all five are usually present in varying degrees. Beyond presence or absence, it is the change in relational

adorable	deep	hollow	loyal	rough	tight
adventurous	delicate	cuddly	lucky	rowdy	tiny
afraid	delightful	curly	lumpy	royal	tired
amazing	dizzy	curvy	mad	sad	tough
amused	dull	cute	mean	safe	tricky
angry	eager	hopeful	meek	scary	trusting
awesome	embarrassed	horrible	mellow	scratchy	ugly
awful	enchanted	hot	memorable	serious	unlucky
awkward	envious	huge	merry	sharp	unpleasant
beautiful	evil	humble	messy	shiny	unsteady
bold	exciting	hungry	mysterious	shy	upset
boring	fabulous	icky	nasty	sick	useful
bossy	fancy	imaginative	naughty	silent	vast
bouncy	fantastic	impish	nervous	silly	velvety
brave	fast	important	nice	simple	vicious
bright	fat	impossible	numb	sizzling	violent
broken	fluffy	innocent	nutty	sleepy	vivid
bubbly	fresh	intelligent	odd	slow	warm
bumpy	friendly	irritating	overjoyed	small	watery
busy	frightened	jagged	overlooked	smooth	wavy
calm	funny	jazzy	pale	sneaky	weak
careful	fussy	jealous	peaceful	soft	weary
charming	fuzzy	jittery	pesky	stiff	weepy
cheerful	gentle	jolly	plain	stormy	weird
clever	giant	joyous	playful	strange	wet
clumsy	glittering	jumpy	powerful	strong	wide
cold	gloomy	kind	precious	surprised	wiggly
confident	graceful	kooky	pretty	sweet	wild
comfortable	grateful	lazy	prickly	tame	wise
confused	gross	light	proud	tense	witty
courageous	gruesome	little	pushy	terrible	wobbly
creepy	grumpy	lively	puzzled	terrific	wonderful
crisp	happy	lonely	quick	thankful	young
crowded	harsh	lopsided	quiet	thick	youthful
cruel	haunting	loud	ragged	thin	yummy
dandy	heavy	loving	rapid	thoughtful	zany
dark	high	low	rich	tidy	zesty

Figure 4.1 Words for Describing Feelingful Intentions. *Source*: Created by Michele Kaschub & Janice Smith.

balance within each pair that gives rise to music's expressive potential. Let's consider how each principle pair functions.

Motion and Stasis

People move in lots of different ways. They can climb, walk, jump, run, amble or meander. Eventually, they will pause or even completely stop. Music, too, may contain moments of considerable motion, moments of stasis, and moments that are of any degree in between. If we were to use a slider to represent the relational balance for a piece with an A section of running sixteenth notes, it might look like figure 4.2.

Figure 4.2   Relational Balance Favoring Rhythmic Motion. *Source*: Created by Michele Kaschub & Janice Smith.

A slower moving B section might be better represented as shown in figure 4.3.

Figure 4.3   Relational Balance Favoring Rhythmic Stasis. *Source*: Created by Michele Kaschub & Janice Smith.

Most important, the A and B sections are perceived to have more motion or more stasis through comparison to each other. It is important to remember that comparisons are not limited to those made within a single piece but extend to all of the other musical pieces that a listener knows and can reference.

Unity and Variety

People look for patterns in nearly everything. The brain not only finds repetition to be highly satisfying but also seeks novelty to hold its attention in a different way. Most music uses a balance of unity and variety to create comfort as well as pique and hold our interest. While unity and variety can be achieved through any of music's components, striking just the right balance can be tricky. Too much of the same thing may cause a listener to lose interest, just as too many novel ideas may also overwhelm.

Sound and Silence

Sound is ubiquitous in daily life, yet the presence or absence of a particular sound can define the focus of our attention. In some cases, a single type of sound can become so familiar that it begins to function as an "attentional constant." Air circulation devices, humming lights, passing traffic, and other environmental sounds are examples of sounds we often ignore until we notice their absence. In this way, silence plays an important role as it can provide an opportunity to reframe and prioritize what we are hearing.

Consider these two graphic representations of sound (gray) and silence (white). In the upper half of figure 4.4, a brass quintet delivers sound and silence in opposition so that the actions of the group are perceived as a whole. In the lower half of the figure, a shifting balance between sound and silence appears in the Trumpet 2 line against constant sound from the other members of the quintet. This structure may draw the listener to pay closer attention to the ideas delivered by the second trumpet while the supporting ideas offered by the remainder of the group assume more of a background position. These are just two of many ways that sound and silence can be shaped to influence how we feel as we engage with music.

Trumpet 1												
Trumpet 2												
Fr. Horn												
Trombone												
Tuba												

Trumpet 1												
Trumpet 2												
Fr. Horn												
Trombone												
Tuba												

Figure 4.4 Relational Sound and Silence. *Source*: Created by Michele Kaschub & Janice Smith.

Tension and Release

Apprehension, excitement, and maybe a little nervousness often precede big life events. Such events are often followed by a certain sense of relief. Music, too, can offer parallel experiences as tension grows and releases through the way sounds are shaped. Like unity and variety, nearly any aspect of music can be shaped to invite tension or provide release. A gradually expanding instrumentation, a steadily building dynamic, or a halting rhythmic figure embedded within a repetitive rhythmic framework can all produce tension and each can be countered to provide release in equal measure.

Stability and Instability

Finally, when life unfolds as expected, we feel stable and safe. But when there are surprises or challenges, we can begin to feel unsettled. Music, too, can have moments of stability or feel unsettled as it searches for firm ground. Music that extends too far into stability or instability is generally considered unpleasant. Stability quickly becomes tedious as there is nothing new to sustain attention and curiosity, while instability grows tiresome as the listener has to work too hard to stay engaged. Striking just the right balance between familiar and novel is a challenged pursued by composers in every genre.

Developing the Capacity of Musical Expressivity

Music teachers often focus on the elements of music (dynamics, form, harmony, melody, texture, tone color, and rhythm) as a means of making performances more expressive. Ironically, focusing exclusively on the elements in creating new music can lead to a lack of artistry. For example, asking a student to create a piece that contains a tempo change may allow the teacher to determine whether or not the student understands the concept of tempo, but the inclusion of a tempo change in and of itself does not guarantee that the music will evoke a feelingful response.

Framing the compositional task in a manner that connects experience and feeling is a more effective approach. For example, a student might be invited to create a piece of music that unfolds like climbing up a slide, and then sliding down. As the very young composers think about what it is like to climb and consider how sliding is experienced in the body, they are likely to explore form and changing tempo in a way that both reveals their conceptual understandings and leads to the creation of a work that features motion–stasis, tension–release, and perhaps other principles, too. In this way, the elements are not artificially strung together but emerge as a natural part of the bigger picture that allows for expressive music to be made.

It is important to help students discover overarching, feelingful intentions, and musical expressivities, as well as how those capacities present themselves within the work. The M.U.S.T.S. can be applied at the level of the whole composition, to just a section of the work, or even across a single phrase or measure. In creating the "climbing and sliding music" described above, a composer might aim to create a composition that builds from a very stable, almost static beginning to a tension-filled climatic conclusion. Within that framework, there might be a section of the piece built on repetition at ever increasing dynamic levels and faster tempos. The melody for that section might feature a series of rising pitch motives that help create the feeling of tension as they climb. Thus tension, and most likely its subsequent release, occurs at the level of the whole composition, the section, and the phrase. Multilevel application may not suit all compositions, but students can be encouraged to think about the M.U.S.T.S. to maximize the expressive potential of their music as is appropriate to their particular goals.

Artistic Craftsmanship

Artistic craftsmanship is the capacity to purposefully shape and organize sounds in a musically expressive manner that invites feelingful response. Composers need to familiarize themselves with a wide range of tools and master a considerable body of techniques to develop fluency in artistic craftsmanship, but this takes time and careful guidance. When techniques are taught before feelingful intentions and musical expressivities have been considered, the compositional process becomes a mere technical exercise.

Very young composers provided with a lesson on range can create a piece of music that explores high and low pitches, but they may not be moved to use those pitches in an artistic manner. Conversely, if the very young composers working on the bunny-inspired pieces use a bass xylophone to recall the bunny hopping, a small glockenspiel played with three mallets at once to parallel the bunny nibbling on food, and an alto metallophone melody for the bunny taking a nap, the teacher can introduce range and tone clusters as compositional tools. Teaching composition with a focus on capacities provides opportunities for discovery. Students can be led to see a connection between specific techniques and their feelingful and expressive impact. This promotes artistry and artistic thinking.

The phrase "tools and techniques of artistic craftsmanship" will appear throughout *Experiencing Music Composition*. "Tools" are those internal and external devices that influence and shape how very young composers think. Internal tools include musical imagination and inner hearing. Activities that encourage students to imagine the sound and ways to manipulate those sounds foster the skill that allows composers to work without external sound sources. Similarly, systems that enable the imagination of sound through the use of symbols for pitch (solfeggio) or time (counting systems) also facilitate the composers' abilities to organize and shape sound in their minds.

External compositional tools include anything external to the composer that helps facilitate thinking. This may include instruments; computers; voices; smart devices; software, applications, or web-based programs; lined and unlined manuscript paper; iconic, invented, or standardized notational systems; and recording devices. Tool choices change and evolve over time to suit the needs of the composer and the music being created. It is important that students experience a wide range of internal and external tools as they develop their personal vocabularies of composition.

"Technique" is the manner in which composers shape sound. It includes choices and decisions about how to use pitch, time, space, dynamics, form, instrumentation and orchestration, texture, and articulation. Technique is best developed through exposure, recognition and purposeful introduction as well as through singing, playing, listening or improvising, and compositional experimentation.

Techniques and Etudes for Grades K–2

While it is beyond the scope of this volume to address all of the possible techniques that very young composers may encounter or utilize in their work, the following material will foster the development of artistic craftsmanship. The etudes suggested below range from initial explorations for first-time composers to more advanced challenges suitable for experienced second-grade students. Etudes serve to teach students about techniques outside of the act of composing. Very young composers benefit from instruction that introduces etudes once they have expressed an interest in particular technique or perceived a "need to know" moment in their own work.

Much of the work of K–2 composers is exploratory in nature. Acquiring a sonic vocabulary is a vital part of the very young composer's development.

The following labels are used to indicate the level of difficulty for each etude. However, the teacher needs to be aware that while some of these may arise spontaneously during play, the very young composer may not be developmentally ready to use them with deliberate intention. Techniques used spontaneously by five-year-olds can sometimes be used intentionally by second graders who have had composing experiences.

(B) Beginner level etudes are appropriate for students with little to no previous composing experience and the very youngest students

(I) Intermediate level etudes are appropriate for students with some previous experience with large group compositions.

(A) Advanced level etudes contain more challenging techniques for experienced composers who are beginning to work on their own or with a partner.

Pitch

Very young composers should be encouraged to experiment and play with different modes, melodic constructs, and harmonies as a way to understand the impact of pitch on how music is experienced. However, this should be in a playful, spontaneous context and not instructional based. For example, Orff instruments (by removing or adding bars) and some music technology programs can be set up to use different scales and modes. Children can then explore using these alternative tonalities.

Modes
1. Create compositions using invented, pentatonic, and other scales (B)
2. Use a single mode throughout a piece (I)

Melodies
1. Invent a motive (B) and repeat or vary it throughout a piece (I)
2. Explore five different melodic shapes: pitches moving up, pitches moving down, smile (high to low to high), frown (low to high to low), and same (intervals remain static) (B)
3. Experiment with different types of motion—steps, skips, or leaps (B)
4. Intentionally remove notes from a melody—truncation (A) Note: very young composers can be quite reluctant to *intentionally* leave out parts of a melody
5. Alter a melody by substituting different pitches or replacing pitches with rests (A)

Harmony
1. Explore the use of more than one sound at the same time (B) using two or more unpitched sounds and then one pitched and one unpitched (I)
2. Explore using two pitched sounds at the same time (I) and one after the other (B)
3. Make up a melody over a drone or other ostinato (I)

Time

Time is an organizing component of the musical experience used to measure the rate and duration of sounds. Musical time is revealed in the way beats are grouped metrically and subdivided to create rhythm. Composers also shape how we experience time through the use of tempo. Below are some ideas for exploring beat, meter, rhythm, and tempo. All require a certain amount of beat competency from very young composers, that is, the ability to maintain a pulse that matches another person or instrument.

Beat
1. Explore music with and without a steady beat (B)
2. Create music with strong and weak beats in predictable and unpredictable patterns (I)

Meter
1. Create music in simple and/or compound meters (B/I)
2. Intentionally use multiple meters in a single work (A) (primarily switching between duple and triple)

Rhythm
1. Create simple and complex rhythms (B)
2. Create rhythmic as accompaniment figures (B)
3. Layer rhythms to create percussion pieces (I)

Tempo
1. Explore how tempo changes can impact the mood or feelingful character of a work (B)
2. Incorporate multiple tempos within a single work (I)
3. Explore nuanced changes in tempo through intentional use of accelerando, rallentando and rubato (I)

Space

Composers do not always control the spaces in which their compositions will be heard. However, composers may specify the ways in which performers are intended to position pieces and the ways that audiences should encounter them. Composers may give special thought to the locations in which their works will be performed, how performers will be physically placed within concert spaces, the mindset that performers and audiences might adopt when engaging with a work, and even storylines that imply other times and places. Some of these considerations are listed below.

Auditory Parameters
1. Create instructions that direct performers to multiple locations within a performance space to alter audience perceptions, that is, on stage, off stage, in the classroom, in the hallway, in a closet, on the playground, at the top of the slide, while swinging, and so on.

Conceptual Spaces
1. Specify a performance space to capitalize on connotations that people bring to the space, that is, the rowdiness of a school playground versus the quiet of a library (I)
2. Dictate program notes that invoke a particular time, space, or set of conditions to frame a musical work or the audiences' experience of the work (B)

Performance Environment
1. Specify the set-up for a concert environment: performers on stage and listeners in the audience (B)
2. Create instructions that require a participatory environment in which performers and listeners intermingle so that audience is part of the performance (B)
3. Create a work to be experienced through earbuds in an individual environment (B)

Temporal Space
1. Create an "extra-temporal" timeline through the use of program notes or lyrics that describe another time/space and seek to transport the audience into that world (I), for example, a song about the first American Thanksgiving or a winter holiday in a different country.

Dynamics

Dynamic levels within a work mark important changes in intensity and do not refer to decibel levels (volume). Changes in dynamics may be achieved in several different ways and influence how music is shaped by performers and experienced by listeners. Composers can manipulate dynamics by altering intensity, relationship, and balance.

Intensity
1. Create varying degrees of intensity by changing written/performed dynamic levels (B)
2. Explore changes in instrumentation: the more instruments, voices or other sound sources contributing to a soundscape, the greater the intensity of the music (B)
3. Use different combinations of instruments, voices or other sound sources to capitalize on natural acoustic properties, that is, children's voices produce sound waves that travel differently than do the sound waves generated by a bass drum (I)

Relational
1. Offer sudden changes in character of the music through the use of subito dynamics, that is, *sfz*—subito forzando, "suddenly with force" (B)
2. Create gradual changes in character of the music through the use of *crescendo* and *decrescendo* (B)

Balance and Blend
1. Specify different dynamic levels for each instrument to increase or decrease presence within texture (A)

Form

Musical form refers to the overall architecture of musical sounds. Organization levels can be viewed from large structures (i.e., symphonies), to mid-level components (i.e., the "A" section), or smaller structures (i.e., phrases). The formal constructs below are listed from smallest to largest in scope.

Motive
1. Create a melodic motive of at least four pitches and then explore the ways it may be varied by altering only the rhythm (I)
2. Explore how the impact of a rhythmic motive is altered when pitches are added—within a single pitch class, close intervals, distant intervals, and so on (A)

Phrase
1. Extend a motive into a phrase through the use of sequence, motivic variation, or other elongation techniques (A)
2. Transform a motive into an imitative gesture by passing it between two instruments or voices (I)
3. Experiment with varying the ending of the phrase to create different feelings—question, answer, uncertainty, surprise, and so on. (A)

Period
1. Experiment with half cadences as a way of joining phrases to build periods (A)

Section
1. Construct different formal structures such AB, ABA, AAB, ABB, Rondo, and other forms (I)

Movement
1. Compose several shorter works with some unifying aspect that allows them to be grouped together into a longer work (A)

Full Work
1. Consider the classification of the work identifying the specific genre, particular style, or performance practice (A)
2. Draw connections between multiple works (A)

Instrumentation & Orchestration

Instrumentation is the choice of particular sounds or combination of sounds while orchestration refers to the way the instruments are used to create particular moods. Once a composer has selected instruments, orchestration may be more specifically tailored to invite a particular affective response.

Sound Sources
1. Explore as many different sounds as possible. Introduce instruments new to the students and allow time for exploration of the possibilities (B)
2. Select instruments, voices, or other sound sources to be used in music composition and explain why each was chosen for inclusion (B)
3. Compose pieces for solo instrument, voice, or other sound source to focus on its particular abilities and idiomatic tendencies (A)

Timbre
1. Explore the different qualities of an individual instrument, voice or other sound sources in terms of character and quality (I)
2. Combine two or more instruments, voices, or other sound sources to explore the interrelationships between different characters and qualities of sound (B)

Range
1. Experiment with the full range of pitches (highest to lowest) available for a single or combination of instruments, voices, or other sound sources to determine the impact of outer margins versus center (B)

Register
1. Create music that capitalizes on the tone quality of a particular instrument, voice, or other sound sources (B)
2. Explore how different instruments, voices, or sound sources take on different qualities in different registers and how this influences combinations of instruments, voices or other sound sources (A)

Tessitura
1. Compose music within a range of pitches that are appropriate—easy to produce and pleasant sounding) to specific instruments, voices, or other sound sources (I)
2. Purposefully create music with pitches that are within the capacity, but beyond the "comfort zone," of specific instruments, voices, or other sound sources (A)

Texture

Texture refers to layers of sound. Texture may include how many independent and dependent musical lines are present, how many instruments or voices are in use, how many sounds are unfolding simultaneously, and the relative presence or absence of particular sounds in the piece at any given moment. Below are a few activities that explore different types of texture.

Monophonic
1. Create unaccompanied melodies for solo and unison parts (B)
2. Compose pieces that contrast unison sections with other textures. (A)

Biphonic
1. Create works with two distinct parts: one line is melodic, the other is simpler and serves as accompaniment (B)

Homophonic Movement
1. Create works with two or more parts moving in identical rhythm, but with different pitches to imply chordal harmony on xylophones or other mallet instruments (B)
2. Create works for solo instruments with simple chordal accompaniment (A)

Polyphonic Movement
1. Create simple rounds and canons beginning with those based on one chord (A)

Articulation

Articulation refers to the way that musical sounds start and end. The use of specific attack and release types can contribute to the distinctive character of the musical style.

Attack
1. Experiment with different ways of producing a sound, that is, staccato, accent, tenuto, marcato, pluck, slap, hard versus soft mallets, and so on. (I)

Movement
1. Explore different ways of ending sounds, that is, pizzicato, damped, fade out, and so on. (I)

Developing the Capacity of Artistic Craftsmanship

Any of the preceding techniques of artistic craftsmanship can be taught as the need arises within the context of a composer's own work or as part of a class focusing on a specific tool or technique. In class settings, short lessons on new concepts or tools are often an effective way of moving a group of very young composers forward to new possibilities. Such introductions should always be soundly based. The students' own performances or recordings can be used to illustrate new compositional ideas and to bring into consideration how such ideas can be used to achieve expressive ends. Students can also be shown how such ideas might be notated in invented, iconographic, or traditional notation. By developing ear and eye together, students expand their compositional palette.

FINAL THOUGHTS

The capacities of feelingful intention, musical expressivity, and artistic craftsmanship may be discussed at nearly any point in the compositional process. The key point is that each can be brought into the conscious thought of very young musicians to help them to develop their ideas and to grow as composers. These capacities help students move beyond the "fortuitous accident" stage where they occasionally, and unintentionally, generate a satisfying musical idea to the point where they create by design. When students consider and deliberately use the M.U.S.T.S. in their work, the tools and techniques they use serve as the sonic connection between lived experience and feeling. Those feelingful relationships often free very young composers to think expressively about music composition so that they may create artistic and personally meaningful work.

Chapter 5

Using *Sketchpages*

GUIDING THE JOURNEY

Have you ever taken a walk in an unfamiliar place and wondered if you would ever find your way? Composers often experience a similar degree of concern as they attempt to travel from musical idea to musical work. Within *Experiencing Music Composition*, compositional paths are illuminated through the use of *Sketchpages*—projectable/reproducible student guides that combine open doodle space, thinking prompts, and composer's notebooks.

Sketchpages accompany every lesson in this volume. They are designed to help students explore their musical ideas as they consider the connections between feelingful intention, musical expressivity, and artistic craftsmanship. The pages serve as inspirational spaces where students jot ideas during or between composing sessions. These ideas become points of reference and help students monitor their progress from initial imaginings through the final product. *Sketchpages* may be added to or revised by students as their compositional journey unfolds. Most important, the use of *Sketchpages* can remove the pressure to arrive at an end product too quickly.

The main purpose of a *Sketchpage* is to provide a practical tool that composers can use to explore and develop the potential of their musical ideas. *Sketchpages* can be particularly helpful when teachers and students discuss musical ideas that primarily exist in the student's imagination. They offer a visual representation of key compositional ideas and relationships. This allows composers to pursue their preferred working styles.

Each segment on the "A-side" of a *Sketchpage* corresponds to a compositional capacity. This allows teachers and students to begin with any capacity and connect outward toward the remaining two capacities. Whether composers are working with images or words, or using invented or traditional notation, *Sketchpages* can be used to capture compositional ideas ranging from motives to fully articulated, large-scale works. This helps composers manage the details of music creation in a productive manner.

The "B-side" of each *Sketchpage* can be tailored to match the notational skill level of young composers. In the appendices of this volume, there are four notation sheets which can be copied onto the back of *Sketchpages* or kept in piles where students may simply collect the sheet they need as they work. The invented notation page is primarily white space. The transitions sheet has both white space for invented notation and staff paper to use as students learn to notate their ideas. The final sheet is staff paper and suited to students who are comfortable with notating their ideas in the traditional manner. Most K–2 composers will use the first or second version.

INTRODUCING *SKETCHPAGES* TO VERY YOUNG COMPOSERS

The best way to introduce the use of *Sketchpages* to very young composers is to facilitate a teacher-guided whole class composition activity. Whole group activities begin with the teacher projecting the *Sketchpage* so that all students can see it and work on it together. The teacher describes the composition task and invites students to discuss each of the guiding questions or prompts while noting student ideas and answers on the *Sketchpage*. With a little guidance, students will be able to work through a *Sketchpage* with a partner, in a small group, and eventually, by themselves.

When students first begin to use *Sketchpages*, they are likely to create simple one-to-one relationships in which they identify a single feelingful intention fulfilled through one of the principle pairs (M.U.S.T.S.) and crafted through the use of one or two techniques. Figure 5.1 is a transcription of a piece created by a student contributing to a class musical collage entitled "Things That Happen in the Fall." The observation of a squirrel taking a cookie from a picnic table was the point of inspiration. The student described his feelingful intention as "mischievous," sought to express that through the use of motion and stasis, and crafted the music with eighth notes and half notes played with legato and staccato articulations. Figure 5.2 shows a graphic representation of these relationships.

Stealing a Cookie

Figure 5.1 Stealing a Cookie. *Source*: Created by Michele Kaschub & Janice Smith.

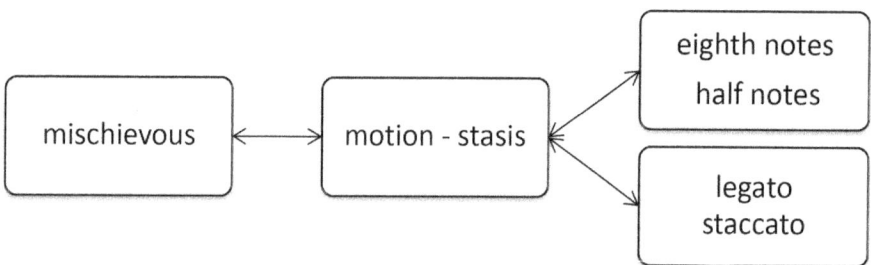

Figure 5.2 Representation of Simple Relationship between Capacities. *Source*: Created by Michele Kaschub & Janice Smith.

As student compositions become increasingly multifaceted, graphic representations of their works can reveal an ever-expanding array of connections. Figure 5.3 shows two diagrams of intermediate complexity while figure 5.4 reveals the complex interconnections of a much more advanced work. While this level of complexity is probably beyond the level of most very young composers, they are included here for teachers to understand the process. Regardless of how simple or complex the connections between capacities may be, *Sketchpages* move learning forward.

SKETCHPAGES AS MULTITASKERS

Sketchpages can fill many roles as teachers and students work together in the classroom. Teachers can use *Sketchpages* to develop a better understanding of each student's needs as young composers use the graphic organizers to help them move musical ideas from their imaginations into the world. With very young composers this usually means drawings and lines that may not assume much meaning until the teacher asks the student about the sketch. Suddenly then, the composer's ideas come into focus.

Using Sketchpages 29

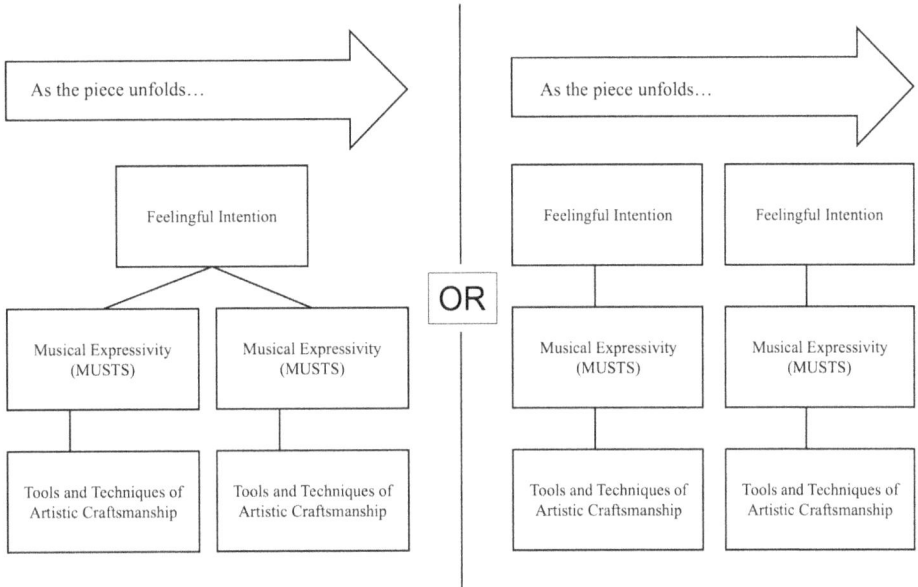

Figure 5.3 Graphic Representations of Intermediate Relationship Complexity among Capacities. *Source*: Created by Michele Kaschub & Janice Smith.

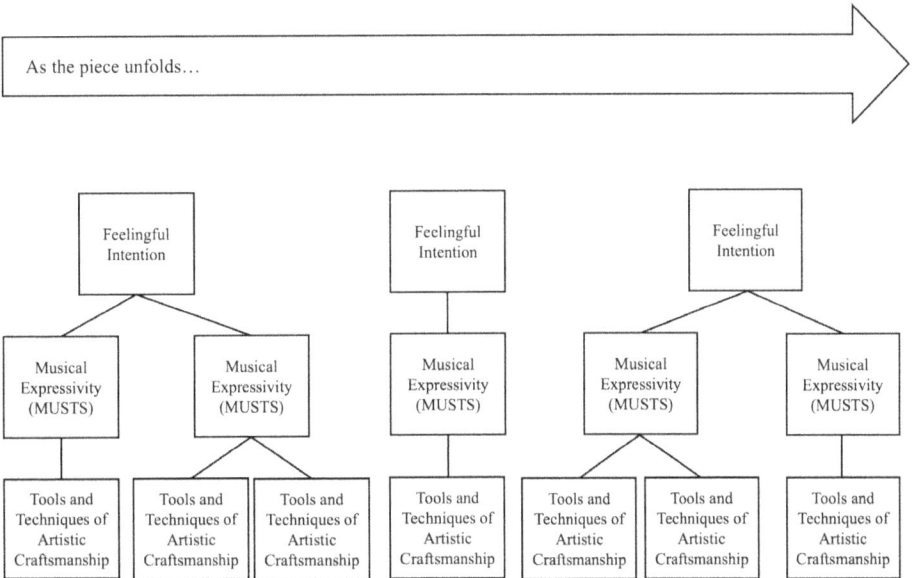

Figure 5.4 Complex Graphic Organizer Representing Highly Complex Relationship among Capacities. *Source*: Created by Michele Kaschub & Janice Smith.

Teachers can use *Sketchpages* to

1. facilitate the development of each child's compositional capacities,
2. encourage the development of critical and creative thinking skills as students imagine, execute and reflect on their compositional ideas,
3. gain a better understanding of each student's compositional processes,
4. provide meaningful and specific feedback reflective of the student's compositional goals, and
5. assess student work (in collaboration with the composer).

Students can use *Sketchpages* to

1. remember key ideas and concepts essential to their feelingful intent,
2. understand the relationship between feelingful intent, musical expressivities/M.U.S.T.S., and the tools of artistic craftsmanship,
3. apply their knowledge and skills to develop and extend initial ideas and conceptions,
4. analyze problems and consider multiple solutions to a broad range of compositional challenges,
5. evaluate a plan for solo, partnered, small group, or large group work,
6. isolate specific compositional challenges, and
7. create expressive compositions that invite performers and audiences to meaningfully engage with music.

Section 3

CREATIVE POSITIVE COMPOSITIONAL EXPERIENCES

Chapter 6

Composition Requires a Different Kind of Teaching

The music that young composers create represents a deeply personal investment and may reveal an unguarded sharing of feelings and emotions. This creates a potentially fragile learning environment. Teachers must make every effort to establish and maintain learning spaces that are supportive and encouraging so that every child feels safe as music is shared and feedback is given.

Kaschub and Smith, 2017

Teaching composition is different from teaching performance or leading listening lessons. Making something new is a little more creative and a little more chaotic than reproducing or describing something that already exists. When teaching composition as we advocate in the *Experiencing Music Composition* approach, the end product is not known when the lesson begins.

In both listening and performance lessons, the teacher knows, and often controls, what the end result will be. The teacher usually determines how pieces are supposed to sound and identifies the knowledge that students should acquire. In composition classes, the lack of a preconceived product requires teachers to trust themselves and their students. They are engaging in a process where learning and its products will naturally emerge over time.

The *Experiencing Music Composition* approach has its foundations in discovery learning and in the constructivist approach to learning. Springing from the work of Jerome Bruner,[1] Jean Piaget,[2] and John Dewey,[3] the central tenet of the approach involves engaging students in activities that pose authentic challenges within a specific domain. The students draw on their own experiences and prior knowledge as they consider how to address these challenges. Because students take the lead in defining problems, testing solutions, and making decisions about which actions to pursue, they become strongly invested in the learning process. This investment is integral to the achievement of compositional success. Similarly, the manner in which teachers approach tasks also greatly influences student learning.

Like their students, most teachers know much more about music composition than they think they do. Teachers know what makes a singable melody, how to vary a motive, and how changing tone colors may alter the character of a musical idea. Creating lists of techniques and specifying how they should be applied may enable the crafting of a product, but it does so at the cost of student ownership and autonomy. However, these are necessary ingredients for individual artistry, creativity, and personal growth to emerge from their work.

Here are two teaching scenarios that illustrate why the teacher's approach matters.

Scenario 1: Mr Izzo's First Apple Song Project

Mr. Izzo's first-grade music classes have all visited an apple orchard. He has decided to have them make up songs about apples. He finds a verse about apples that falls neatly into a duple rhythm with only quarter notes and eight notes and writes it on the board.

> Bright red apples on a tree
> Some for you and some for me
> Climb the ladder, not too high
> We'll make applesauce and pie.

He sets up an alto xylophone with just the pitches C, D, E, and G and a mallet to play them. He also sets up a recording device to capture the children's ideas.

The class begins by reading the poem and clapping the rhythm. They gradually figure out the notation for the rhythms and Mr. Izzo notates the rhythm above the words. Next he invites them to use the xylophone to make up a tune and turn the poem into a song. He tells the class they must start and end their tune on C, but they can play anything they want for the rest of the song. Volunteers eagerly raise their hands. Mr. Izzo turns on the recording device and asks the class to quietly chant the poem while their friends take their turns. Most of the children take a turn creating a "song" on the instrument.

That evening Mr. Izzo listens to the recordings. Figure 6.1 is the rubric he designed to assess their work.

	With ease	As expected	With difficulty	Not yet
Started and ended on C	Yes, both	Yes, start only	Yes, end only	No
Matched the rhythm of the words	Always	Mostly	Sometimes	No
Good melody	Conjunct melody	Singable	A few big leaps	Random notes
Overall musical effect	Excellent	Very Good	Acceptable	Poor

Figure 6.1 Mr. Izzo's Rubric. *Source*: Created by Michele Kaschub & Janice Smith.

As he listens to the pieces, he notices many similarities in the pieces. Nearly all the pieces start with *C, D, E* and end on *E, D, C*. Many students seem to have trouble staying with the chanting class while they make up their tunes. Some students seem to just randomly choose notes to play. Overall, their pieces lack musicality and expressivity. Mr. Izzo selects several of the better ones to notate. The students will sing these during the next class and add instrumental accompaniments.

Scenario 2: Mr. Izzo's Apple Song Project

Mr. Izzo's first-grade music classes have all visited an apple orchard. He has decided to have them make up class songs about apples. He begins class by talking with the students about their trip and about all the things they have been learning about apples. He lists keywords from their conversation on the board.

Once a lengthy list of what the students know about apples and about their field trip has been created, Mr. Izzo displays the *Sketchpage* in figure 6.2 as he suggests that the class write an apple song.

He begins by asking the class what they would like their song to be about and pointing to the list of ideas they have generated. Since the ideas seem to cluster around three things—the trip, what can be made from apples, and apples themselves—he suggests the song should be about one of those ideas. The class picks the topic of picking apples by making suggestions and then voting.

Figure 6.2 *Source*: Created by Michele Kaschub & Janice Smith.

Mr. Izzo then asks the class to think about how it feels to pick apples. The class mentions that it is a little scary to climb a ladder but easy to pick the ones they can reach standing on the ground. Mr. Izzo adds "safe, then scary, then safe" to the first apple on the class *Sketchpage*. Mr. Izzo then asks how music would start out that was about standing on the ground picking apples. The children talk about happy melodies and calm sounds. He then asked how climbing the ladder would sound and the children talked about the music being slower going upward and then slowly coming back down.

Mr. Izzo suggests that maybe their apple song might have three parts and writes ABA on the third apple. He asks the children how they can make up music that shows three parts. They suggest medium fast, then slower, then medium fast again, and they suggest the middle needs an upward melody and then a downward melody. They also mention making the middle scary on the way up and down but not quite so scary while picking the apples. The children want to use short sounds for picking the apples. Mr. Izzo notes their ideas on the sketch page and then moves on to other materials.

Later that evening Mr. Izzo crafts some possible lyrics for the class's song.

For the A sections he uses:

> Bright red apples on a tree
> Some for you and some for me
> Climb the ladder, not too high
> We'll make applesauce and pie.

For the B section he creates:

> Up the ladder, way up high
> Climbing slowly toward the sky
> Picking apples, 1, 2, 3
> Juicy fruit for you and me.
> Down the ladder, now I go
> Being safe, I take it slow.

At the start of the next class Mr. Izzo reviews their *Sketchpage* with the class and confirms their ideas for the song. He then shares his ideas for words. They chant the words several times in different rhythms and select one they like the best. This also helps them learn the words. Mr. Izzo has the class imagine melody for the two lines in their heads. After a few seconds, he asks them to plug their ears and sing their melody lines out loud. He sings also to encourage them to make sounds. He repeats those instructions several times while wandering around the room listening for singable melodies and sketching them on paper.

Next he asks if anyone wants to share their song. Several eager hands go up. (If no one volunteers, Mr. Izzo sings one of the tunes he sketched as he was listening to them sing.) Each of those children sings their tune and the class echoes the tune afterward. Eventually Mr. Izzo guides the class to select one of the ideas that seems particularly suitable. They repeat the process for the next two lines and the A section is complete.

During the following class, they follow a similar process to make up the B section. Mr. Izzo creates a chart that has visual clues for how the music sounds and also makes a traditionally notated copy of the song for each child to take home. The students rehearse the song and add small percussion instruments to it. They perform it for the other first grades at "Morning Meeting" when all the first-grade classes gather to start the day.

Each of the first grades has a song to perform and they are all quite different from one another. One is about making and eating applesauce. Another is about the art project the class did by using apples sliced in half to make prints. Another is about the hidden star in the apple's core. The last one is about the different kinds and colors of apples.

Later, after all the classes have finished crafting, rehearsing, and recording their pieces, Mr. Izzo listens to the performances. He is delighted to hear how unique each one is. He notices that the classes have contrasted their A and B sections in numerous ways. Different classes have explored dynamics, instrumentation, major and minor, tempo and more.

Mr. Izzo decides to play some of the recordings of the pieces for the classes during the next lesson. He will engage them in discussions to see if the students seem to be understanding more about making music expressive by asking questions about how the songs made them feel and what in the music made them feel that way. He will guide the learning by focusing on the feelingful intention behind each piece and the M.U.S.T.S.

Mr. Izzo's students created interesting songs because they were asked questions that invited them to think about what they wanted to share. He asked what they experienced and how that might be expressed in music. He also provided a bit of help with how they might do that artistically. Mr. Izzo could have had the class create the words to the songs if he had the time; a classroom teacher might have helped the students write a poem about the experience and shared it with Mr. Izzo. There are many possibilities for how this activity could be done. The important thing is that the ideas come from the children with the assistance of the teacher—and not the other way around. By asking questions, teachers guide students to contribute their own ideas to the project. After some experiences with models of whole class composing, very young composers are better prepared to work alone and in small groups on other composition projects.

WORKING WITH "IN-PROCESS" COMPOSERS

Sometimes it is difficult to trust that students will come up with ideas. However, the process of composing is quite similar to the experiences children have when they engage in storytelling. Given time and a little encouragement, they eventually find an idea and get underway. One particular challenge in music composition is that students often have musical ideas in their heads that they cannot articulate or perform. This is where the teacher can help by prompting students to think critically about what they are imagining.

Asking questions that evoke imaginative responses often helps students take steps toward getting started or advancing a germinal idea. For example, when students are creating a piece for classroom instruments, ask them to close their eyes and imagine themselves performing on stage while an audience sits and listens. Wait a few seconds and then add that everyone claps enthusiastically when the performance has ended. Ask the students to describe the piece they imagined.[4] Jot these thoughts down for the students on a *Sketchpage*.

Another example of evoking imagination might be:

Imagine that an artist has come to you and asked you to compose the music for her new cartoon show. The main character is going to be "Indu, the Ninja Cat." How would the theme music for a ninja cat sound? How does it feel to be a ninja cat? How does a ninja cat move? Can you hum or sing the music?

The technique of using questions to prompt student action requires knowledge of the students and what might be blocking their creativity. Some students will simply state what their problem is, while others may have a hard time figuring it out. Some students have a very clear idea of what they want their music to sound like, but they cannot figure out how to make (or notate) the sounds. Other students are simply shy, or hesitant to share their ideas. While these situations can be frustrating for students and teachers alike, they are temporary and will resolve with practice and supportive guidance. Let's consider two key points in the process when students are likely to get stuck and ask for help.

Idea Generation

Students often wonder where to begin their pieces. There is no correct answer for this question. The *Sketchpages* provided with each lesson present multiple entry points to each project. It is important to remember that every composer will find an individual entry point of comfort. For some composers, this will be a feeling or mood. Other composers may select an instrument or quickly discover a melodic or rhythmic fragment that sets the stage for the use of specific compositional techniques. Regardless of where and how the process starts, encourage students to think about the connections between all three capacities to enhance the overall quality of their work.

Idea Development or Extension

Once young composers have a work in progress, ask questions about what should come next. The teacher must ask questions and not be too quick to offer suggestions. It is easy to share solutions that are obvious to you as a "quick fix" and this does save class time. However, it is more beneficial to the students to figure out the answers. The guideline should be: whenever possible, ask – don't tell.

Listen to a recording of the piece and be prepared to listen more than once. Repeated listenings can be facilitated by saying, "Let's hear our piece again. Maybe we can get a better idea of what should come next." Once you have a clearer sense of what has been created, discuss the work with the composers using the following questions as is appropriate:

1. What was the feeling we were trying to create?
2. How were we trying to capture that feeling?
3. Is there something specific that we are trying to do?
4. What have we tried in an attempt to solve the current challenge?
5. Are there other things we might try?
6. Would you like me to offer a few options for us to try to see if they help us find what we are after?

As much as is possible, follow the students' lead in the discussion. Save the offer of presenting options as a final resort for times when students are truly at a loss for what to do or when you are modeling for the whole class. When presenting options, present at least three and make sure that the composers know that they do not have to use any of the presented options. The options are simply shared in hopes of spurring further exploration and idea trials to prompt student thinking.

ANCHORING KNOWLEDGE, INVITING INSPIRATION

Another way to help students gain independence within the compositional process is to make a wide variety of resources available to them. Brief playlists organized by topic, genre, style, compositional techniques, or other categorizations can provide auditory inspiration to composers facing specific challenges. Likewise, visual quick reference tools can serve to remind students of what they know or allow them to make important connections that further their work.

In the scenarios that appear in the opening of Section 3, Mr. Izzo could have gestured toward posters of the M.U.S.T.S. that his class might reference as they decided how their pieces might sound. He might have added to these charts during the final discussion of the pieces. These posters are called "Anchor Charts" and they are created from student observations of how music works. As students listen to music, sing songs, or play instruments, teachers can invite them to notice and discuss compositional gestures. The techniques that they observe can then be recorded on posters, webpages, or other easily accessed locations, "anchoring" what has been learned for students to reference as they carry out their own compositional work.

While teachers can make and post resource charts ahead of time to facilitate learning, student-created charts constitute the most powerful tools because students feel a personal investment in the information represented. Each chart will be unique as it reflects what the students of a particular compositional community have discovered and analyzed together. Similarly, anchor charts do not have a set format. Rather, each chart evolves as teachers and students work together to document what they have discovered about a topic, tool, or idea. A quick Internet search for "music anchor chart" turns up a vast array of designs. Anchor charts may be focused on any capacity, may be organized by musical expressivities (M.U.S.T.S.), or include definitions of key concepts, lists of ideas, or steps in the process. The requirement common to all anchor charts is that they must be helpful to the students who will use them. An example of a completed anchor chart is shown in figure 6.3.

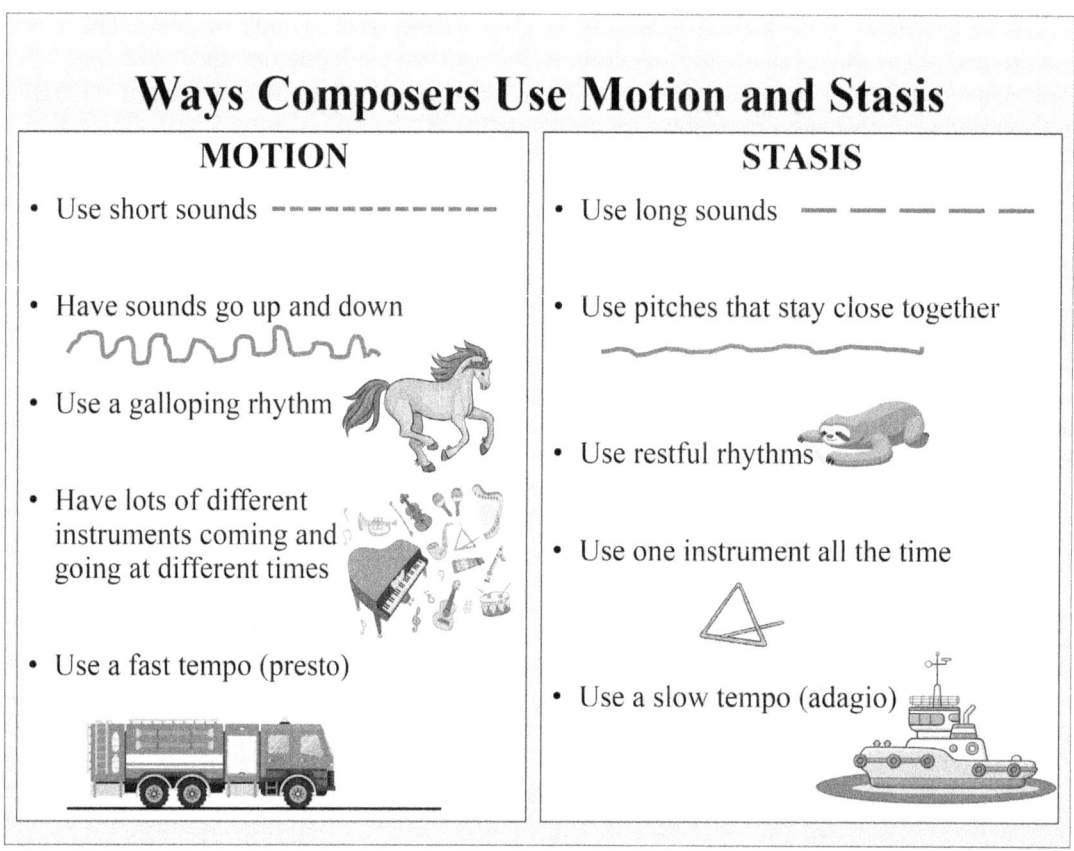

Figure 6.3 *Source*: Created by Michele Kaschub & Janice Smith with images from iStock/Credit: rosinka, flowerstock, mountainbrothers, Bullet_Chained, Ghrzuzudu.

GUIDELINES FOR SHARING COMPOSITIONS—
GIVING AND RECEIVING FEEDBACK

Sharing compositions for feedback allows students the opportunity to improve their work while it is still in progress. It can happen in whole class composing if the teacher records the work in progress and plays it back to the class. This can give them direct insight as to how an audience may react and allows the students to critically reflect on their own work and the works of others. As composers share music with each other they discover new musical ideas, different ways of achieving particular outcomes, and compositional techniques that may be of use to them in the moment or in the future. Playing the pieces written by one class of young composers for another class—without revealing who the composers are—can often help generate more ideas.

In addition to musical skills, composers also develop enhanced communication skills as they speak about their works. They also learn to offer specific praise and appropriate critique to their peers. As their experiences with composition and presentation grow, they gain confidence in their ability to describe their intentions. They become increasingly able to describe their working processes and they recognize the ongoing development of their compositional capacities. To foster this growth, teachers must create and maintain an environment that allows students to feel safe in sharing work.

Setting Expectations and Creating Guidelines

Before students can offer feedback on the compositions of their peers, they need an opportunity to think about how they will feel as they receive comments. Teachers can invite students to imagine sharing a composition with their classmates and prompt them to think about the type of feedback that they would hope to receive. Students should also consider how they would like comments made.

Begin with a composition model created by the teacher or another class. Have students practice offering praise and constructive feedback. Use the statements made by the students as examples to put together a list of guidelines, such as those shown in figure 6.4, to help students provide useful feedback in a pleasant and supportive manner.

- Be kind.
- Offer praise.
- Be specific.
- Talk about what the composers asked listeners to comment on.
- Use "I" words.
    - I think_____ worked for me because_____.
    - The use of_____ made me feel_____.
    - As I listened to your piece, I learned that_____.
    - I'm wondering if you tried_____? I ask because_____.
    - Maybe you could try_____ because it_____.
    - I'm curious about_____. Can you tell us why_____?

Figure 6.4 Tips for Composers Offering Feedback. *Source*: Created by Michele Kaschub & Janice Smith.

It is also important for composers to think about how they will accept feedback. It can be difficult to listen to what others have to say about work that you are deeply connected to and perhaps quite proud of. However, composers benefit from experiences that require them to gain some objective distance from their music so that they can thoughtfully evaluate what is working and what may need further work. Figure 6.5 outlines a few thoughts that composers should keep in mind as they listen to feedback.

- Listen.
- Be open to ideas that you don't think you like at first.
- Suggestions are only suggestions. You do not have to change your music.
- Listen to praise and enjoy it.

Figure 6.5 Tips for Composers Receiving Feedback. *Source*: Created by Michele Kaschub & Janice Smith.

Composer's Circles

Composer's Circles are gatherings of composers, teachers, performers, and others who may provide useful feedback on compositions in progress or completed works. Circles often involve whole classes when composition projects have been completed as a whole class or in small groups, and it may also be limited in size with just three to five composers who listen to each other's work and offer constructive commentary.

It is important that teachers facilitate initial Composer's Circles so that students learn how to fill the roles of presenter and responder. Circles typically begin with a composer, or group of composers, introducing a piece. In the case of whole class compositions from another class, the teacher can provide the introduction and should share any information that may be relevant to the listeners. This may include information about inspiration, feelingful intentions, musical expressivities, techniques being used, or problems that the composers were seeking to address. Figure 6.6 shows some statements that may help teachers of very young composers introduce their work.

- The piece that the class was working on is called _____.
- They were trying to create the feeling of _____.
- They have used (M.U.S.T.S) to try to invite a feeling of _____.
- The first musical idea that they tried _____.
- They have tried using (technique) to _____, but found out that _____.
- They are hoping that someone might have a suggestion for how they could _____.
- Please tell me *what* you think works and *why* you think it works for you.

Figure 6.6 Following the Composer's Lead. *Source*: Created by Michele Kaschub & Janice Smith.

Once the introduction has been given and the audience has heard the work, the teacher should encourage students to offer constructive criticisms. It is helpful to invite praise and criticism in balance—two praise comments to each comment of constructive criticism. As students become comfortable with this process and gain confidence as composers, the balance of comments may be adjusted to suit the needs of each composer as is shown in the written comment form of figure 6.7. The same chart is also useful when assessing works created by the whole class.

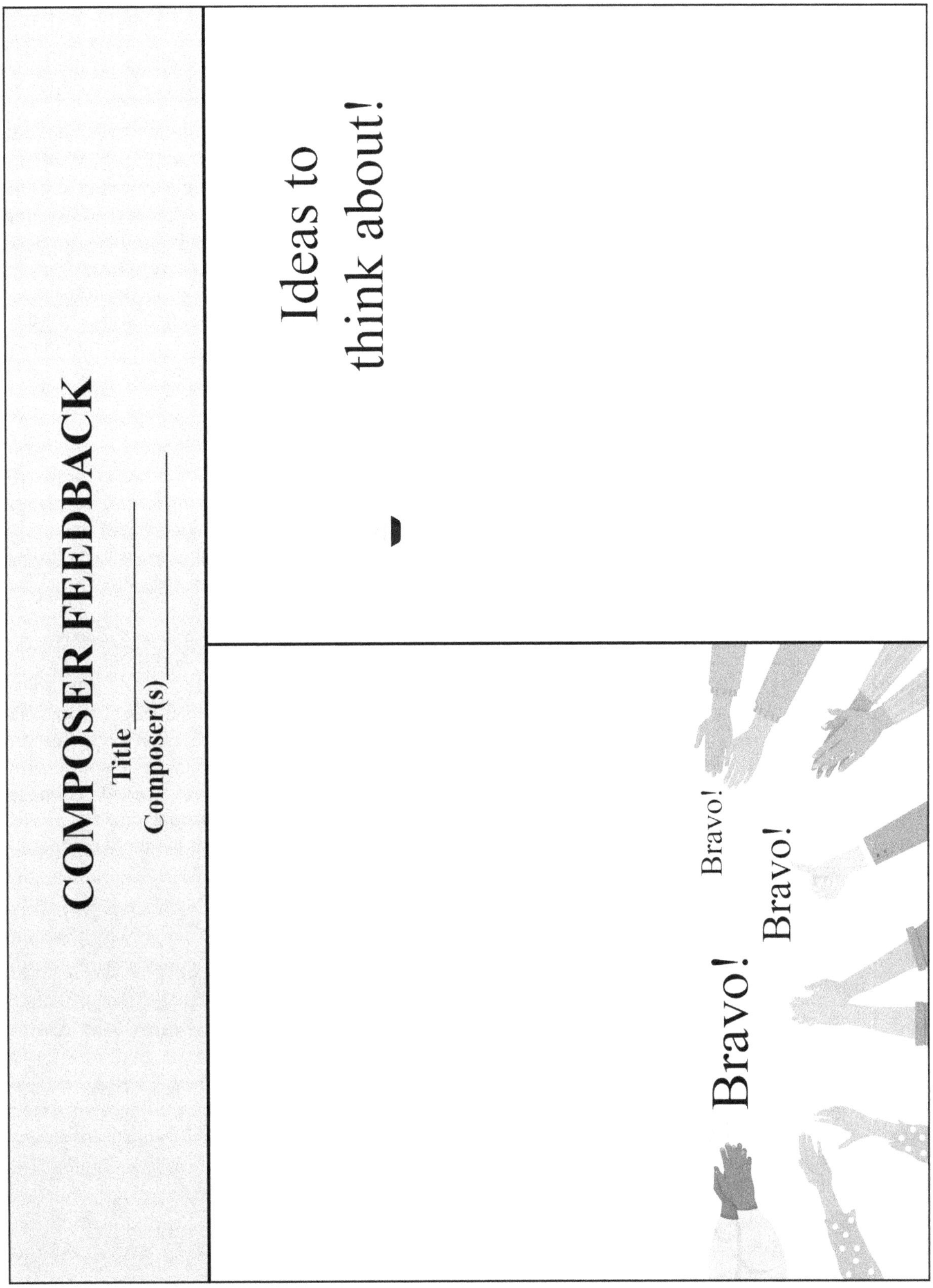

Figure 6.7 *Source:* Created by Michele Kaschub & Janice Smith with images from iStock/Credit: designer29 and primo-piano.

Working with Reluctant Sharers

Unfortunately, some very young composers may be reluctant to share what they have created. They may not even want to share their composition with friends or the teacher. In such cases, it is important to respect the very young composer's reluctance while continuing to show interest in what he or she is doing. Working as a whole class or in pairs or groups is usually helpful for these students.

Composers who do not receive feedback on their work are unlikely to further develop their compositional capacities. Therefore, it is important to find ways to provide feedback to reluctant sharers as soon as possible. Some students will agree to participate in one-on-one conferences, either with the teacher or a friend within the class. Others will be comfortable with recording their compositions so that the teacher can listen to them apart from the students. In this situation, feedback in early interactions must offer valid praise with only a few minor criticisms. This will help students overcome the fear of criticism while allowing some productive feedback to be given.

As trust grows, students can gently be led into participation in the Composer's Circle. Interaction should begin with reluctant sharers being invited to offer suggestions, but not expected to share their own work or that of their group. By participating in this way, their confidence may grow and they may begin to feel emotionally safe within the group. Once trust has been established, reluctant sharers may become more willing to present their music for feedback.

Putting Feedback to Good Use

The feedback that very young composers receive from the teacher or peers within the Composer's Circle holds varying potential. Very young composers often put the ideas presented to them to immediate use if they are working on a composition that is still in progress, but they are far less likely to apply suggestions to a finished work. However, when facilitating whole class compositions, teachers should try to elicit suggestions from the class members rather than offering their own feedback.

Encouraging students to revise work that they consider completed requires a cautious approach. Educational researcher Sandra Stauffer has suggested that students do not spontaneously revise their works until sometime around age eleven.[5] Prior to that, when the child has completed the piece, he or she is finished with it and ready to move on to the next thing. Mentors can make suggestions like, "Do you think there might be another part to it?" However, young composers may not agree and wish to start a new work. It is important to respect their developmental stage while continuing to suggest ways revision might work. Students may be more open to suggestions for revisions if those suggestions further their own artistic intentions as were spelled out on the *Sketchpage*. Suggestions for revisions to whole class compositions may be possible after some time has passed and the class is more experienced. They may be willing to revisit a "finished" work, but more often prefer to move on to something else.

Post-performance Reflections

As students share the final versions of their pieces, teachers should facilitate questioning that reveals multiple feelingful intentions, each of the musical expressivities, and the tools and techniques of artistic craftsmanship. Multiple capacities unfold in every piece. Taking time to identify them and discuss how they work reveals music's complex constructions and potentials for expressive artistry.

Moreover, some children will discover new things about their own compositions as they describe them and as they hear the observations made by those who have listened to their work. Other children will recognize their own techniques and processes only when they hear similar ones described by their peers. Allowing the processes of composition to be experienced, observed, and discussed presents myriad entry points for young composers to learn more about themselves and the art of composition.

MAKING THE MOST OF LIMITED TIMEFRAMES

In the ever-present battle against the clock, class time is seldom given to the creation and sharing of compositions. Yet considerable learning occurs when students analyze and discuss what they have observed in the compositions of others. In just 2–3 minutes, pairs of students can identify and draw connections between the feelingful intentions, musical expressivities, and the techniques of artistic craftsmanship used within a short piece *if* that process has repeatedly been modeled by the teacher with music experienced in class. In just 3–5 minutes, small groups of students can describe how the choice of feelingful intentions and use of compositional techniques were designed to engage a particular audience or bring about a specific type of reaction. Brief and focused analysis and discussion help students hone their skills of perception so that they become increasingly aware of the tools and techniques available to them as they work to artistically craft music for expressive purposes. This is time well invested.

NOTES

1. Bruner, J. S. (1961). "The act of discovery." *Harvard Educational Review* 31 (1): 21–32.
2. Piaget, J. (1936). *Origins of intelligence in the child.* London: Routledge & Kegan Paul.
3. Dewey, J. (1938). *Experience & Education.* New York, NY: Kappa Delta Pi.
4. Deutsch, D. (2012) Teaching gifted learners in composition. In Kaschub, M. and Smith, J. (Eds.) Composing our future: Preparing music educators to teach composition. NY: Oxford University Press, p. 136.
5. Stauffer, S. L. (1998). *Children as composers: Changes over time.* Paper presented at the biennial convention of the Music Educators National Conference, April 1998, Phoenix, AZ.

Section 4

TEACHER GUIDES AND STUDENT *SKETCHPAGES*

Chapter 7

Teacher Guides and Student *Sketchpages*

This section contains fifteen teacher guides designed to help you mentor primary grade students as they explore composition. Each guide includes

1. an overview of a composition project;
2. the identification of one or more *National Arts Standards for Music* that will be addressed within the project;
3. descriptions of how to facilitate student learning throughout the compositional process;
4. examples of questions that can be used to prompt the development of compositional capacities; and
5. one or more *Sketchpages* for students to use as they create original compositions within each project. These may be projected for the whole class to view or used as handouts when children need to draw or add to the sheets. Some sheets are to be copied and cut for use as manipulables.

CURRICULAR ORGANIZATION

Projects are organized by the suggested grade level across the five different compositional genres. Throughout each strand, very young composers will consider the feelingful intentions, the musical expressivities, and the tools and techniques of artistic craftsmanship that suit a particular genre and project. They also will explore their creative potential as composers and come to value their own interpretations and understandings of what makes their music artful and important.

	Songwriting	*Composition & Visual Media*	*Instrumental Music*	*Electronic Music & Digital Media*	*Music Theater*
K	Teddy Bear Lullabies	Sonifying Characters: The Gingerbread Man	Stormy Weather	Achieving Artistry with Apps	Birthday Wishes
Gr.1	Field Trip Song	Background Music for Storytelling	Duets with Two Sounds: A Musical Conversation	Sound Blocks and Patterns	Making a "When I Grow Up, I Want to Be" Song
Gr.2	A Song for Grandparent's Day	Exploring Leitmotif: The Mitten	Chamber Music Trios	Terrific Textures	Incidental Music for Puppet Theater

Songwriting

The creation of songs is often one of the first compositional activities that children pursue. As the voice tends to be the primary instrument of very young composers, the song is a natural outlet for musical thinking. Songs also lend themselves to the structure of stories—another creative medium that children warmly embrace. The three lesson projects featured in this book invite very young composers to think about songs that express wishes, songs about field trips or traveling, and songs for special family members.

Composition and Visual Media

Music often plays a supportive, yet critical, role in how we experience stories. In the composition and visual media strand of the *Experiencing Music Composition* curriculum, students create (1) music for a familiar story with one prominent character and a large supporting cast; (2) a story with a common theme, but a wide variety of variations; and (3) stories with a variety of characters, each of which has their own leitmotif or theme.

Instrumental Music

Many music teachers have used instruments with very young composers to create soundscapes and impressionistic weather-based pieces. The first lesson in this section adds the dimension of feelingful intention to these pieces by planning how the sounds will suggest the feeling of a storm. After several whole class activities, it is usually time to move into working in pairs to create instrumental duets. The book *Max Found Two Sticks* by Brian J. Pinkney can serve as a focus for creating a duet with one pitched and one unpitched instrument. These duets can then lead naturally to chamber music trios with one pitched instrument and two unpitched ones. Advanced very young composers may be able to create percussion canons based on rhythms they create, and possibly notate, if they understand a system of rhythmic notation. This usually requires some skill in singing while staying on a part in a round. Advanced second graders may be able to do this, but it is more typical of third or fourth graders.

Electronic Music and Digital Media

While experts differ in their approval of using technology with very young children, we feel there are appropriate and interesting ways to use technology that lead to valuable insights for young composers. The projects included in this volume use (1) sound exploration to experiment with unity and variety; (2) building blocks of sound to graphically notate ideas; and (3) layering sounds in ways that make them fit together in musical ways. All three could be done without technology, with a variety of devices and a variety of applications, or with online programs.

Music Theater

One of the easiest ways to begin to create an understanding of how music is used in theater is to create a few "I Am" songs in the context of familiar events that can be based in reality or expanded by imagination. A simple beginning step is in the lesson "I'm the Star of My Birthday."

As a connection to the broader world, students also can create songs about their family and friends. By adding an overture, incidental music, and a song for each character, very young composers can create puppet theater plays that become mini-musicals.

PROJECTS FOR KINDERGARTEN

Chapter 8

Teddy Bear Lullabies
Songwriting

About this Project

Music teachers often teach a unit on lullabies to very young children. Lessons may include listening to and singing lullabies from many cultures that share common qualities such as soothing sounds, quiet tones, gentle motions, and so on. Once an understanding of the nature of lullabies is established, it can be fun for children to make up their own lullabies. These can be assembled into a class recording and shared with parents.

To create an authentic setting for the creation of lullabies, place a child-sized rocking chair in the front of the room, and encourage children to bring in their teddy bears or other favorite cuddling toys. This activity might be coordinated with classroom teachers to take advantage of "pajama days," or a time when students are studying hibernation or some other sleep-related topic.

National Arts Standards for Music: Creating

This lesson presents students with an opportunity to do the following:

Imagine
- MU:Cr1.1.Ka With guidance, explore and experience music concepts (such as beat and melodic contour).
- MU:Cr1.1.Kb With guidance, generate musical ideas (such as movements or motives).

Plan and Make
- MU:Cr2.1.Ka With guidance, demonstrate and choose favorite musical ideas.
- MU:Cr2.1.Kb With guidance, organize personal musical ideas using iconic notation and/or recording technology.

Evaluate and Refine
- MU:Cr3.1.Ka With guidance, apply personal, peer, and teacher feedback in refining personal musical ideas.

Present
- MU:Cr3.2.Ka With guidance, demonstrate a final version of personal musical ideas to peers.

Materials

- *Sketchpage*
- Tools: Voices, recording device, rocking chair, extra teddy bears, and other stuffed animals for those who did not bring one to class

Project Time

- It will take approximately five minutes per child to complete this project.

DISCUSSION QUESTIONS TO DEVELOP COMPOSITIONAL CAPACITIES

? Feelingful Intention—How do lullabies usually make you feel?
? Musical Expressivity—How does that feeling sound? How can you make your voice sound that way?
? Artistic Craftsmanship—How will your lullaby sound? What words will you use?

SEQUENCE OF ACTIVITIES

- Review qualities of lullabies the children have learned to sing. Ask the very young composers questions like: How do lullabies usually make you feel? What about the music that helps you feel that way? How can we use our voices to help our teddy bears fall asleep? (Imagine)
- Talk also about how one might sing the lullaby differently if Teddy did not want to go to sleep and how the lullaby might change as the teddy bear settled down. End with something like: "How might our voices sound once Teddy was sound asleep?" (Imagine)
- Review the questions on the *Sketchpage*. Make a list of words and vocables that very young composers might use in their lullabies. Draw on the words from the other lullabies that they know: hush, go to sleep, doo doo doo, lulla lulla, and so on.
- Have the children hold their bears and hum a little tune to them—all at the same time. The teacher models as well. Ask them to try to come up with a tune they like. Repeat this process two or three times. Guide the students with these suggestions: (Plan and Make)

  Make up a lullaby for your Teddy Bear.
  Practice singing your lullaby, until it is just right. (Evaluate and Refine)
  When you are ready, we will record you singing to your bear. (Present)

- Encourage the children to try to put a few words to their tunes.
- Invite volunteers to sit in the "composer's chair"* and sing their songs. Use the rocking chair for this and record the children's creations. Remind the students that they can choose how to begin and how to end their lullabies. (Present)
- The lesson can stop here. However, it can be beneficial for students to do some reflection on their lullabies during the next music class. Play recordings of several of the students' lullabies that seemed evocative and lead a discussion about why they were effective. (Evaluate)

Optional Extension

When a child in the class has a new sibling, do this as a whole class activity to create a lullaby for the new baby. Create a personalized lullaby for the new baby, rehearse it, and record a performance to share with the parents.

---

* Our thanks to Dr. Daniel Deutsch for the composer's chair name and idea.

Source: Created by Michele Kaschub & Janice Smith with images from iStock/Credit: julos, gavni, Ralers, Maksym Chechel, and ~Userba9fe9ab_931.

Chapter 9

Sonifying Characters: The Gingerbread Man
Composing and Visual Media

About This Project

In this lesson, students will design a sound story. They will experience each of the compositional capacities and discover rondo forms from the music they create. This activity can be done as a whole class project over several classes. Another approach is to have individual students make up songs for the different animals. This can be accomplished by using only vocal sounds, so the activity can be done in many different settings. It also makes an intriguing "informance" piece to share with parents or to make available as an audio file on a classroom website.

National Arts Standards for Music: Creating

This lesson presents students with an opportunity to:

Imagine
- MU:Cr1.1.Ka With guidance, explore and experience music concepts (such as beat and melodic contour).
- MU:Cr1.1.Kb With guidance, generate musical ideas (such as movements or motives).

Plan and Make
- MU:Cr2.1.Ka With guidance, demonstrate and choose favorite musical ideas.
- MU:Cr2.1.Kb With guidance, organize personal musical ideas using iconic notation and/or recording technology.

Evaluate and Refine
- MU:Cr3.1.Ka With guidance, apply personal, peer, and teacher feedback in refining personal musical ideas.

Present
- MU:Cr3.2.Ka With guidance, demonstrate a final version of personal musical ideas to peers.

Materials

- Two *Sketchpages* to project; print and cut-out animal images.
- It is helpful to have a story book to share with children; alternatively, the teacher can simply tell the story to the class being sure to repeat the gingerbread man's response and to have a phrase for each of the animals to say as the gingerbread man runs by them. One possibility is *Classic Children's Fairy Tales: The Gingerbread Man,* illustrated by Gail Yerrill, Parragon Books, 2012.

Project Time

- It will take approximately forty minutes to create the completed story. This project can take place over several lessons or be done in one class.

DISCUSSION QUESTIONS TO DEVELOP COMPOSITIONAL CAPACITIES

? Feelingful Intention—What feeling matches the animal?
? Musical Expressivity—How would the feeling sound?
? Artistic Craftsmanship—How can we make the animal's sounds into a song for the animal?

SEQUENCE OF ACTIVITIES

- Begin the lesson by teaching the children a refrain for the Gingerbread Man.
- Read the story and make a list of all the animals that the Gingerbread boy meets as he runs away from the old couple.
- How does the Gingerbread Man feel? Do his feelings ever change? When?
- Have the class create a theme for the Gingerbread Man using the text from the story:

    Run, run, run as fast as you can.
    You can't catch me, I'm the Gingerbread Man. (Imagine, Plan and Make)

- Optional other words, depending on the version of the storybook you are using:

    I ran from the farmer, and from his wife, too
    You can't catch me, not any of you.

- Discuss the music that might be created for each animal. How does each of the animals feel? Even though they have some of the same feelings, how might they sound different? (A horse might be quite different from a pig.) How does the fox feel differently than the other animals? How will that sound? Additional animals can be added to the story as needed. The lesson is effective with only the three animals, especially if this is a whole class activity. The Yerrill version above has only a cow, pig, and horse. Other versions may include a dog and a cat. The children can suggest other animals. (Imagine)
- Have individual students take turns creating short songs for the animals that appear as the story unfolds or have the whole class create each song. Use vocables for animal sounds and the text from the book. A cow might sing some version of "Moo, moo, moo. I want to eat you." These words can be repeated to make a short song. (Plan and Make)
- For a whole class version, teach the words to the children and repeat them several times. Then have everyone imagine a tune in their heads for the song. Alternatively, have them all make up a tune and sing out loud all at the same time. Listen for a musical idea and select one. Have the whole class sing that tune several times and record it to aid in remembering it. Then move on to the next animal and repeat the process. Be sure to review how this animal might sound differently and why. (Plan and Make)
- For individual contributions, omit the "sing aloud at the same time" step, and ask for volunteers to sing their "cow song" using the words the class has been repeating. Listen to several possibilities and select one. Rehearse it with everyone singing it and record it. Then go on to the next animal.
- Help the very young composers focus on the feelingful changes when the fox enters the story. Should the music for the fox sound different than the music for other animals? How is his song different? What other sounds might enhance this part of the story? Create a theme song for the fox. (Imagine, Plan and Make)

- Perform the story with music. If possible, have one child narrate. Other children may sing the animal songs or play other sounds (splashing water of the river, running of the fox, snap of the fox's mouth, etc.), and everyone can sing the refrain. (Present)
- Ask students for suggestions about improving the music.

   Prompting question: What could we do differently to make our music more interesting? (Evaluate and Refine)

- Perform the story again using the suggested revisions. Repeat as needed or as time permits. (Present)

Optional Extensions

- One alternative is for the teacher to make up the gingerbread man's song and teach it to the class. The very young composers then create the rest of the songs. This saves time and can mean that the whole lesson can be completed in one class.
- It is also fun to perform the music without narration. Record the "purely musical" performance. Listen to the recording and help the children identify the patterning that comprises the rondo form.
- Add other sounds as appropriate near the end. Plastic bottles partially filled with water can make an effective river sound. Create "river shakers" by using a 1-liter bottle filled one-quarter to one-third of the way full with water. Glue the cap onto the bottle. Two pieces of wood or a wood block make a satisfying "snap" when the gingerbread man meets his demise. Scary underscoring via a technological device can add to the river scene. All of this can be done vocally as well.
- Make up songs with no words. Use vocables of the animal sounds, but make them into tunes.
- Create an ending song:

   He ran, ran, ran as fast as he could.
   He ran through the fields, and he ran through the wood.
   But he came to a river, and he met a bad friend,
   And that's how the gingerbread man met his sad end.

Source: Created by Michele Kaschub & Janice Smith with images from iStock/Credit: julos and ksena32.

What animals will I meet?

How does each animal feel about meeting (eating) me?

What kind of song will each animal sing when I run by?

Does the fox feel differently than the other animals?

What kind of song will the fox sing?

Source: Created by Michele Kaschub & Janice Smith with images from iStock/Credit: zhev and koya79.

Source: Created by Michele Kaschub & Janice Smith with images from iStock/Credit: julos.

Sonifying Characters: The Gingerbread Man 61

Source: Created by Michele Kaschub & Janice Smith with images from iStock/Credit: julos, zhev, and koya79.

Chapter 10

Stormy Weather

Instrumental Music

About This Project

With very young composers, it is often best to begin with as few prerequisites as possible. "Stormy Weather" requires little preparation. The students need to know what a thunderstorm is like, but even that can be easily reviewed through classroom discussion. Children often come to school knowing that music usually has a beginning, a middle, and an end. For this lesson to be successful, they need to be able to follow directions in a group setting. Beyond that, little else is necessary. Students will learn the typical conducting gestures for "cue," "crescendo," "decrescendo," and "cut off." They will experiment with the available sounds to create a musical thunderstorm.

National Arts Standards for Music: Creating

This lesson presents students with an opportunity to:

Imagine
- MU:Cr1.1.Ka With guidance, explore and experience music concepts (such as beat and melodic contour).
- MU:Cr1.1.Kb With guidance, generate musical ideas (such as movements or motives).

Plan and Make
- MU:Cr2.1.Ka With guidance, demonstrate and choose favorite musical ideas.
- MU:Cr2.1.Kb With guidance, organize personal musical ideas using iconic notation and/or recording technology.

Evaluate and Refine
- MU:Cr3.1.Ka With guidance, apply personal, peer, and teacher feedback in refining personal musical ideas.

Present
- MU:Cr3.2.Ka With guidance, demonstrate a final version of personal musical ideas to peers.

Materials
- *Sketchpage*
- Tools
  - Instruments to create the effect of raindrops, thunder, wind.
    Hand drums, rain sticks, suspended cymbal and soft mallets, classroom timpani, or other large deep sounding drum.

- Have a sound maker for each child in the class if you are using instruments.
- Alternatively, this can be done with voices and body percussion. Rubbing thighs, rubbing palms of hands together, patting legs, snapping fingers, tapping on surfaces, clapping, stamping, and vocal wind sounds all can have a place in a thunderstorm piece.

Project Time

- It will take approximately twenty minutes to complete this composition activity.

DISCUSSION QUESTIONS TO DEVELOP COMPOSITIONAL CAPACITIES

? Feelingful Intention—How does it feel when it looks like it is going to rain? How does it feel when you are in the middle of a thunderstorm? How does it feel as the storm winds down and ends?
? Musical Expressivity—What kind of sounds could we make for each of those feelings?
? Artistic Craftsmanship—Where will we use specific sound sources in our piece?

SEQUENCE OF ACTIVITIES

- Discuss how a thunderstorm begins. After taking several responses, direct the student's attention to the idea that they can start with wind, or only a few drops, but then rapidly increase in intensity. Then guide the conversation to how storms end. Help the class decide that there is a gradual diminishment of rain, and then the sun comes back out. (Imagine)
- Review cueing (by pointing) and cutoffs (demonstrate) and practice starting and stopping. Then teach getting louder and getting quieter by moving palms of hands away from each other or toward each other. This can be practiced by patting their legs or with the instruments if your students have to self-control to not play until they are asked to contribute.
- If you have not already done so, distribute the instruments.
- Give these directions: "When I point to you, begin playing your instrument quietly. When everyone is playing, watch me for the signal to play louder or quieter. Toward the end of our storm, I will look at you and give you a cutoff. You will stop playing one at a time." (Plan and Make)
- After several practice attempts, record the children's efforts and play it back to them. (Present) Discuss what was effective and what might be improved the next time. For example, sudden changes in dynamics are only effective for the thunder and work best if they are spread out over the span of the piece. Usually, we hear only one thunderclap at a time unless there is more than one storm going on. (Evaluate and Refine)
- Invite various children to be the conductor and have the class create more thunderstorms that are recorded and similarly discussed. (Plan and Make)

Optional Extensions

- If you have children who are frightened by loud sounds, this can be done only as a rainstorm.
- *Minds on Music: Composition for Creative and Critical Thinking* by Kaschub and Smith, published by Rowman and Littlefield Education (2009), contains directions for creating classroom snowstorms.
- At another time, consider trying other kinds of storms: hurricanes, tornados, dust storms, and so on.
- A similar type of piece can be created to reflect a sunny day with the sun coming up, various things happening, possibly with a hot spell in the middle where little happens, and then the sun going down.

Source: Created by Michele Kaschub & Janice Smith with images from iStock/Credit: colematt, julos, s-cphoto, and Zalina Dodokhova.

Chapter 11

Achieving Artistry with Apps
Electronic Music and Digital Media

About This Project

This project is about the guided exploration of music creation apps with very young composers. Unlike free play with sound apps, this project is based on creating with an adult or another more experienced person. The adults' role is to scaffold the experience while keeping the focus on playing with sound. It is not necessary to make a finished product, although that may occur. Once very young composers have had experience with creating and manipulating sounds electronically, many of the projects in the book can use those sounds to create music.

National Arts Standards for Music: Creating

This lesson presents students with an opportunity to:

Imagine
- MU:Cr1.1.Ka With guidance, explore and experience music concepts (such as beat and melodic contour).
- MU:Cr1.1.Kb With guidance, generate musical ideas (such as movements or motives).

Plan and Make
- MU:Cr2.1.Ka With guidance, demonstrate and choose favorite musical ideas.
- MU:Cr2.1.Kb With guidance, organize personal musical ideas using iconic notation and/or recording technology.

Evaluate and Refine
- MU:Cr3.1.Ka With guidance, apply personal, peer, and teacher feedback in refining personal musical ideas.

Present
- MU:Cr3.2.Ka With guidance, demonstrate a final version of personal musical ideas to peers.

Materials

- *Sketchpage*
- Some apps to play with:
  - Touch Sounds—for the very youngest
  - Singing fingers—notions of upward and downward motion are helpful
  - Sketch a Song
  - Musyc

- Lily
- Pitch Painter

Project Time

- It can take as long or as little time as the children and adults want to play. In a classroom with a touch screen, a few minutes every class can be plenty over time.
- One-on-one time is rare in a music classroom, but parents can be encouraged to use music apps with their children at home. This can be especially effective after the children have had some experience at school.
- School also provides opportunities to collaborate with other children, which may or may not be available at home.

DISCUSSION QUESTIONS TO DEVELOP COMPOSITIONAL CAPACITIES

These are just a few ideas to get started. More are in the lesson activities below.

? Feelingful Intention—Can you find a funny sound?
? Musical Expressivity—Can you find a sound you like? How does that sound make you feel? Can you make that same sound again?
? Artistic Craftsmanship—Can you make a short sound? A long sound? A higher/lower sound? A louder/quieter sound? Can you make more than one sound at a time? Can you make it faster/slower?

SEQUENCE OF ACTIVITIES

- Select an app from the list above or another of your choosing. Explore its sound potentials and learn how it works. A good beginner one is *Touch Sounds*. This app allows the child to make only one sound at a time, but it also shows the idea of higher equals upward on the screen. Ask questions like:
  - Can you make a shorter sound?
  - Can you make a higher sound?
  - Can you make a funny sound?
  - Have you found a sound you like?
  - Can you find a sound that is the opposite of your favorite one? How might you use them both? (Imagine)
- Find an app that allows more than one sound at a time. *Sketch a Song* and *Pitch Painter* both can do this, as can many others. Create a piece that uses two different sounds.
  - How will the sounds work together? (Plan and Make)
    - What happens if you play the sounds one after the other?
    - What happens if you put them together?
    - Will they take turns?
  - How will your piece sound—will it be funny or sad or triumphant or scary or? (Imagine)
- For any app, try saying, "That is an interesting sound (rhythm, tune) you are using. What else can you do with it?"
- Depending on what you hear the very young composer doing, ask one of these questions:
  - I think I hear a pattern in your piece. Can you tell me about it?
  - Is there anything that repeats in your piece?

The idea is to help the very young composer see that repetition is a good thing, but that variety is needed as well (Evaluate and Refine). Another good idea is to save favorite sounds somewhere for future use. This is a type of audio sketchbook that can be a fruitful source of ideas for more formal composition lessons.

Optional Extensions

For older or more advanced students:

- Find a friend and have a musical conversation without saying anything. Can you ask and answer questions using electronic sounds only?

(A more difficult challenge: See if you can copy part of the question in your answer.)

- While polite people do not both speak at once, musicians often perform at the same time. Can you find a friend and make up music that fits together?
- Sometimes music is interesting when there are very different things going on. Can you make up a very different part to your piece that still fits with it?

Source: Created by Michele Kaschub & Janice Smith with images from iStock/Credit: julos, tomap49, and colematt.

Chapter 12

Birthday Wishes
Music Theater

About This Project

Birthdays are important events in very young children's lives. This project can be an ongoing, year-long project that gets added to each month. Summer birthdays can all be done in June (Or can be done on half birthdays for June in December, July in January and August in February). The class creates an A section to the Birthday Song. As birthdays arise, each child creates his or her own verse for the song. Composing the verses to the Birthday Song becomes another way of making the day special for each child. This project is a combination of whole class and individual composing. The second optional extension suggests a way to make this into a short musical skit.

National Arts Standards for Music: Creating

This lesson presents students with an opportunity to:

Imagine
- MU:Cr1.1.Ka With guidance, explore and experience music concepts (such as beat and melodic contour).
- MU:Cr1.1.Kb With guidance, generate musical ideas (such as movements or motives).

Plan and Make
- MU:Cr2.1.Ka With guidance, demonstrate and choose favorite musical ideas.
- MU:Cr2.1.Kb With guidance, organize personal musical ideas using iconic notation and/or recording technology.

Evaluate and Refine
- MU:Cr3.1.Ka With guidance, apply personal, peer, and teacher feedback in refining personal musical ideas.

Present
- MU:Cr3.2.Ka With guidance, demonstrate a final version of personal musical ideas to peers.

Materials
- *Sketchpages*
- Voices (instruments optional)

Project Time
- It will take approximately ten minutes to complete the project once the project has been defined.

DISCUSSION QUESTIONS TO DEVELOP COMPOSITIONAL CAPACITIES

? Feelingful Intention—How do we feel about receiving presents?
? Musical Expressivity—How might that feeling sound?
? Artistic Craftsmanship—How can we make those feelingful sounds? What sounds might be best for this present?

SEQUENCE OF ACTIVITIES

- Recognize the child who has a birthday that day. (Confirm this with the child's or children's teacher ahead of time, if possible.) Discuss briefly any birthday plans and present wishes. Talk about the difference in feelings between wishing for and receiving the gift.
- During the first time you do this lesson, create a class song for the A section. Record this and notate later so you can recall it the next time you do it.

    It's my birthday the candles are lit
    It's my birthday and I'm wishing for . . .

  Aim to have the A section tune end without a full cadence so that it creates a feeling of being open-ended. (Plan and Make)

- Sing the song and have the birthday child imagine blowing out the candles and sing what he or she is wishing for. This can be a whole class song for reluctant singers, but most young children will willingly participate. (Plan and Make)
- Once the child has stated a wish, encourage the child to make up a B section about the wish. This can be done using words similar to these: (Present)

    I'm wishing for a ____.
    I'm wishing it today.
    I'm wishing for a ____.
    On my birthday.

- Consider concluding the piece with:

    It's my birthday the candles are out
    It's my birthday and I love my . . .

  Use the same material as the original A section but changing it slightly based on the discussion about the difference between wishing for and actually receiving the wish. This time, conclude with a full cadence. With older young composers (late first grade, or second), discuss how this feels different than the first song and why. (Evaluate and Refine)

Optional Extensions

- A classroom chart can be made with each child's name, birthday, and his or her wish. This can be done as a weekly activity or once a month. Teachers can look for an increased ability to create effective B sections over the course of the year. Compare recordings from earlier in the year with later ones.
- Turn this into a short skit. Ask the child and the class to imagine that their wish actually comes true. How would that feel? How might the wish sound? Using instruments if they are available (or body percussion and voices if they are not), create a section for the song that tries to capture that feeling. Have the child pantomime opening the present and then using it, if the child wished for something that is a toy. If the child wishes for something like a visit from a grandparent, act that out and create music to accompany it. This section might be much longer than the other sections. Involve other children as the instrumentalists, sound effects or other actors. Allow the birthday child to select the other performers from those who are willing. If time allows, record the performance and watch it. Ask did our music feel like we thought? Does it need anything else?

Wishing for a _____
Feels like _____
Music sounds like _____
Best sounds to use for this present are _____

Playing with a _____
Feels like _____
Music sounds like _____
Best sounds to use for this present are _____

Source: Created by Michele Kaschub & Janice Smith with images from iStock/Credit: julos and GCapture.

PROJECTS FOR GRADE 1

Chapter 13

Field Trip Song
Songwriting

About This Project

An educational field trip can provide a wealth of material to use for songwriting, and writing a song after a field trip can help solidify the essential learnings the experience was supposed to provide. This is a whole class songwriting activity. The lesson grew out of the yearly field trip first graders took to an orchard in one of the author's schools but has been done with other settings such as a concert hall, a zoo, and an aquarium and could work with many more.

National Arts Standards for Music: Creating

This lesson presents students with an opportunity to:

Imagine
- MU:Cr1.1.1a With limited guidance, create musical ideas (such as answering a musical question) for a specific purpose.
- MU:Cr1.1b With limited guidance, generate musical ideas in multiple tonalities (such as major and minor) and meters (such as duple and triple).

Plan and Make
- MU:Cr2.1.1a With limited guidance, demonstrate and discuss personal reasons for selecting musical ideas that represent expressive intent.
- MU:Cr2.1.1b With limited guidance, use iconic or standard notation and/or recording technology to document and organize personal musical ideas.

Evaluate and Refine
- MU:Cr3.1.1a With limited guidance, discuss and apply personal, peer, and teacher feedback to refine personal musical ideas.

Present
- MU:Cr3.2.1a With limited guidance, convey expressive intent for a specific purpose by presenting a final version of personal musical ideas to peers or informal audience.

Materials

- *Sketchpages*

Project Time

- It will take approximately thirty minutes to complete a song while working as a whole classroom. The project can be done in segments over a few classes but works best when the field trip experience is fresh in the childrens' minds. A verse/chorus form works well, but the song could work as a rondo if that better fits the events of the field trip.

DISCUSSION QUESTIONS TO DEVELOP COMPOSITIONAL CAPACITIES

? Feelingful Intention—How did you feel on the way to the [insert destination]? How did you feel while you were there? How did you feel when you got back?
? Musical Expressivity—How might music for that type of feeling sound?
? Artistic Craftsmanship—What can we do to make the music sound like how we felt while we were on this trip?

SEQUENCE OF ACTIVITIES

- Determine with the classroom teacher what the essential learnings of the experience are. What is it the children are supposed to know as a result of the trip?
- Discuss the trip with the class making simple notes about their comments on a board where they can see it. Ask:
  ○ Where did you go?
  ○ What did you see?
  ○ What did you do?
  ○ What did you learn?
- Using the list, suggest making up a song about the experience.
  ○ Ask how they felt going to the place? How did they feel when they got there? How do they feel about the trip now that it is over? All can be ideas for using in the song. (Imagine)
  ○ Ask the children what was the most important thing they learn and write a phrase for that. For example, in the orchard experience, one essential learning was that orchards are like farms for fruit trees and that tending them is a lot of work. Another one was that apples grow on trees and are harvested only once a year, even though you can find them in the store all the time. (Plan and Make)
  ○ Start by writing the words for a chorus that summarizes the experience and is catchy and easy to remember. It sometimes helps to keep a rhyming dictionary handy for the teacher to use. (Plan and Make)
  ○ At this point, teachers can write the lyrics with the classes or take the ideas and write the lyrics themselves. Here is an example for the orchard trip:

    > We're going on a field trip, we're on the bus today
    > We're going to an orchard, it's not far away.
    > An orchard is a tree farm, a very special kind.
    > We're going to pick apples, and see what else we find.

- Once you have the lyrics created, help the class create the melody. One way to do this is to chant the words out loud all together to establish a rhythm. Try two or three ways and ask the class which they like best. For example, chant it in a simple duple meter, in a compound duple meter, or with syncopations. See figure 13.2 for some examples of how to do this. (Plan and Make)
- Once a meter and rhythm have been established, ask the children to think about how a tune might go for their song. Would it start up high, down low or somewhere in the middle? What shape might the first phrase take—should it go up, down, smile (up-down-up), frown (down-up-down) or stay around the same pitch? Draw the shape they determine above the lyrics. Then ask the class to imagine a tune with that shape in their heads. Invite them to sing it internally a couple of times. Ask for volunteers to sing their tunes out loud and have the whole class echo their ideas. Do this several times and then help the class select one idea to use for this song. Be sure to use a recording device while you do this so that you do not lose one idea when another one is being considered. (Plan and Make)

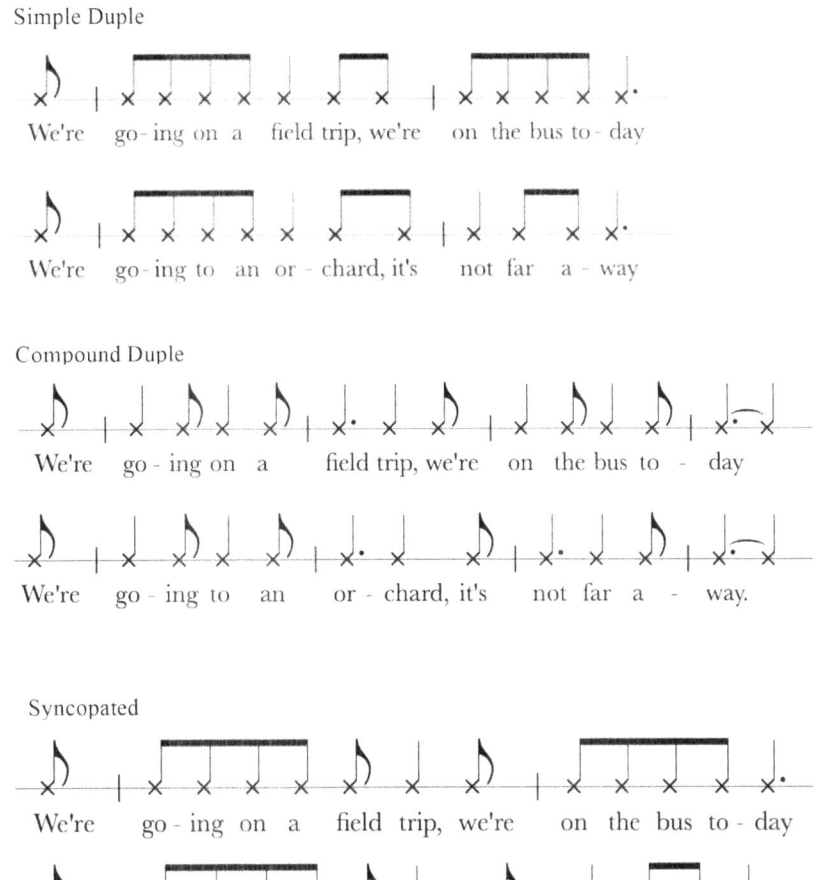

Figure 13.2 Rhythmic Variation of Lyrics. *Source*: Created by Michele Kaschub & Janice Smith.

- If the class has many reluctant singers or no one volunteers, have them plug their ears and sing all at once while you walk around and listen. Then sing several of the tunes you heard for the class and ask them which they prefer. (Evaluate and Refine)
- Proceed to compose the rest of the chorus the same way. As you work, discuss whether any of the lines should have the same tune: Lines one and three? Or two and four? Should any be similar but end differently? Many songs use an AABA[1] or ABCA format. Follow the children's lead. (Evaluate and Refine)
- Once the chorus has been completed, you may wish to move on to something else and come back to this project during the next class.
- Write verses for two to four additional aspects of the trip. (If you are using this idea with older students, teams can create the verses. With K–2, it usually works better to do it all together with the teacher helping to turn the ideas into workable rhymes and musical phrases.) (Plan and Make; Evaluate)
- Practice singing the song until the class can perform it smoothly, then make a recording and share it on a class website. (Present)

Optional Extension

- If several classes visit the same site, have each class create their own song and then share them with the others.
- A short assembly program can be created using the songs and other activities the classroom teachers have done with the children.

Source: Created by Michele Kaschub & Janice Smith with images from iStock/Credit: julos, oasis15, colematt, Inna Karlamova, and designer29.

Chapter 14

Background Music for Storytelling
Composition and Visual Media

About This Project

Creating sound effects and background music for stories is a satisfying way to introduce young children to the very beginning of film scoring. Favorite picture books can be enhanced with a variety of sounds and musical motifs to increase the effectiveness of the story. Once created, a film version can be made and shared. Teachers can guide students to move beyond simply adding sound effects to add background music and themes that help tell the story.

National Arts Standards for Music: Creating

This lesson presents students with an opportunity to:

Imagine
- MU:Cr1.1.1a With limited guidance, create musical ideas (such as answering a musical question) for a specific purpose.
- MU:Cr1.1b With limited guidance, generate musical ideas in multiple tonalities (such as major and minor) and meters (such as duple and triple).

Plan and Make
- MU:Cr2.1.1a With limited guidance, demonstrate and discuss personal reasons for selecting musical ideas that represent expressive intent.
- MU:Cr2.1.1b With limited guidance, use iconic or standard notation and/or recording technology to document and organize personal musical ideas.

Evaluate and Refine
- MU:Cr3.1.1a With limited guidance, discuss and apply personal, peer, and teacher feedback to refine personal musical ideas.

Present
- MU:Cr3.2.1a With limited guidance, convey expressive intent for a specific purpose by presenting a final version of personal musical ideas to peers or informal audience.

Materials
- *Sketchpages*
- Classroom instruments, voices, found sounds, computer sounds, and so on.

Project Time

- It will take approximately 30 minutes to complete.

DISCUSSION QUESTIONS TO DEVELOP COMPOSITIONAL CAPACITIES

? Feelingful Intention—How does this part of the story feel?
? Musical Expressivity—What would music sound like that also felt that way?
? Artistic Craftsmanship—How can we make music that sounds like that?

SEQUENCE OF ACTIVITIES

- Play a short cartoon without any sound and talk about what is missing. How is music used to help tell a story? Lead the discussion to talk about the difference between sound effects and background music. (Imagine)
- Select a favorite story to sonify. Among those that work well are:
  - *Where the Wild Things Are* by Maurice Sendak
  - *Green Eggs and Ham* by Dr. Seuss
  - *Click, Clack Moo: Cows That Type* by Doreen Cronin
  - *Night Animals* by Gianna Marino

However, almost any excellent picture book will do. This activity can also be done with stories the children write. It is important to the process that the children know the story well.

- Using the story you and the children have selected, decide where in the story sound effects could be used to make the story more interesting. Read the story adding those sounds (Plan and Make).
- Then talk about how the story makes the children feel in specific places. Using the questions listed above, determine what kind of music could enhance the story (Imagine). With whatever music making tools are available, create background music for the story in several places. Try to encourage students to create short tunes that capture the mood of the place, character, or action (without adding more sound effects) (Plan and Make).
- Rehearse the story with the music and the sound effects. When the students are ready to perform, create a recording and listen to it. Ask the students to think about their work: What worked well? What might have worked better? Should anything be changed (Present, Evaluate and Refine)?
- Revise and re-record as time allows.

Optional Extension

Listen to a recording of a picture book that has background music and sound effects. Have the children identify examples of both and discuss their effectiveness. If you are using a video of the book, listen to it first without the video and then again after the discussion with the video. When humans focus on what they can see, sometimes they miss what they can hear. Both are important skills to develop and listening without the pictures can help build musical skills.

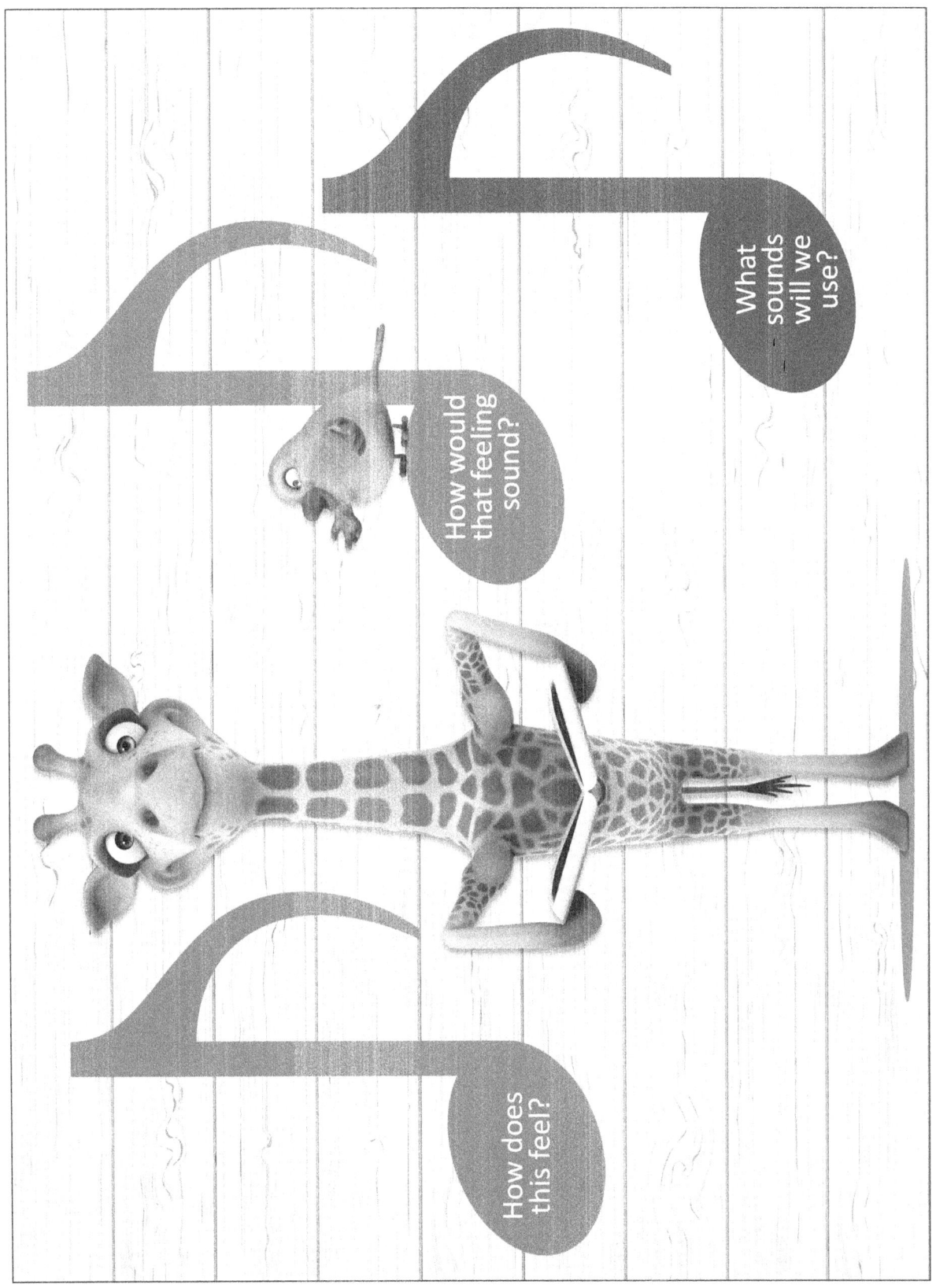

Source: Created by Michele Kaschub & Janice Smith with images from iStock/Credit: julos and Victor_85.

Chapter 15

Duets with Two Sounds: A Musical Conversation
Instrumental Music

About This Project

This project is a simple way to begin working with more than one sound at a time. The lesson starts with a practice activity using cat-like vocalizations in a conversation and then proceeds to planning, creating, and performing an instrumental piece for two unpitched percussion instruments. It is also possible to do this project using body percussion or vocal sounds in settings where instruments are not available. Optional extensions are offered for classes with access to technology or for those who wish to use electronic sound sources or include pitched instruments.

National Arts Standards for Music: Creating

This lesson presents students with an opportunity to:

Imagine
- MU:Cr1.1.1a With limited guidance, create musical ideas (such as answering a musical question) for a specific purpose.
- MU:Cr1.1b With limited guidance, generate musical ideas in multiple tonalities (such as major and minor) and meters (such as duple and triple).

Plan and Make
- MU:Cr2.1.1a With limited guidance, demonstrate and discuss personal reasons for selecting musical ideas that represent expressive intent.
- MU:Cr2.1.1b With limited guidance, use iconic or standard notation and/or recording technology to document and organize personal musical ideas.

Evaluate and Refine
- MU:Cr3.1.1a With limited guidance, discuss and apply personal, peer, and teacher feedback to refine personal musical ideas.

Present
- MU:Cr3.2.1a With limited guidance, convey expressive intent for a specific purpose by presenting a final version of personal musical ideas to peers or informal audience.

Materials

- *Sketchpage*
- Stack of composition cards for each pair of composers
- A wide variety of unpitched percussion instruments grouped by tone colors: drums/woods/metals or organized by how they are played: struck/scraped/shook.

Project Time

- It will take approximately 10 minutes to create and practice the pieces once the preliminary discussion has taken place. The whole process will take approximately thirty minutes.

DISCUSSION QUESTIONS TO DEVELOP COMPOSITIONAL CAPACITIES

? Feelingful Intention—What mood or feeling will you explore? (Hint: Think about a real conversation you might have. What would it be about? How would you feel about talking with another person? Will they feel the same way? Will you create a single feelingful impression for your piece or use more than one?)
? Musical Expressivity—Which of the M.U.S.T.S. will you use? Will your partner use the same ones or different ones?
? Artistic Craftsmanship—How will the instruments interact? Will they take turns? Play at the same time? What else might they do?

SEQUENCE OF ACTIVITIES

- Warning: This project generates quite a bit of sound. You can challenge students to keep their conversations "at a whisper" to reduce the volume in the room.
- Discuss with the class what happens when people have a conversation. Taking turns, listening to the other person and answering thoughtfully, sometimes arguing, sometimes agreeing with what the other said. Point out that people do not usually repeat what the other person has said.
- Have the class experiment with cat conversations. The teacher "speaks" in a cat voice with another person (classroom teacher, teaching assistant, or child). Explain to the class that you will have a conversation about wanting to trade something with the other person—could be a toy or book or even half a sandwich—but can only meow to communicate. Once the class watches the conversation, have them try it for themselves. Offer a different scenario, establish a quiet signal for when to end the activity, and have them take 30 seconds or so to try it. (Imagine)
- Tell the class that they will do something similar with instruments today. Display the *Sketchpage* and talk through the questions. (Imagine, Plan and Make)
- Have the children select partners. This can be the same person with whom they have just conversed as cats or a different person.
- Show the instrument groupings and tell them partners will each pick one instrument from different groups—for example, one drum and one triangle. (Plan and Make)
- Invite students to think about what feeling they want to create for their piece and which instruments might be used to invite that feeling. Students should then select their instruments and a set of composition cards. (Plan and Make)
- Give students eight minutes to create their compositions and lay out their scores. At the end of the eight minutes, give students two minutes to practice and polish their pieces. Plan and Make, Evaluate and Refine)
- Invite each team to perform their composition for the class. If possible, snap a picture of the score and record the composition. (Present)
- After each piece is performed, ask the composers what they believe worked well in their piece. Ask students to describe how the sounds they made matched the feelingful they identified at the beginning of their process. (Evalaute)

Optional Extensions

- Students can later do this project using one pitched and one unpitched instrument. It is often helpful to let the pairs create two pieces so that each child has a turn using the pitched instrument. Composing with a pitched instrument involves creating melodies and is, therefore, a more complex activity. Some young composers will be ready for this based on their previous experiences. This type of piece can become less of a conversation and more of a melody with accompaniment. Encourage students to experiment with both ways of considering a piece.
- Have students experiment with using one acoustic unpitched percussion instrument and one electronic sound source from a tablet or other sound source. How does this change the feeling of the piece?

Duets with Two Sounds: A Musical Conversation

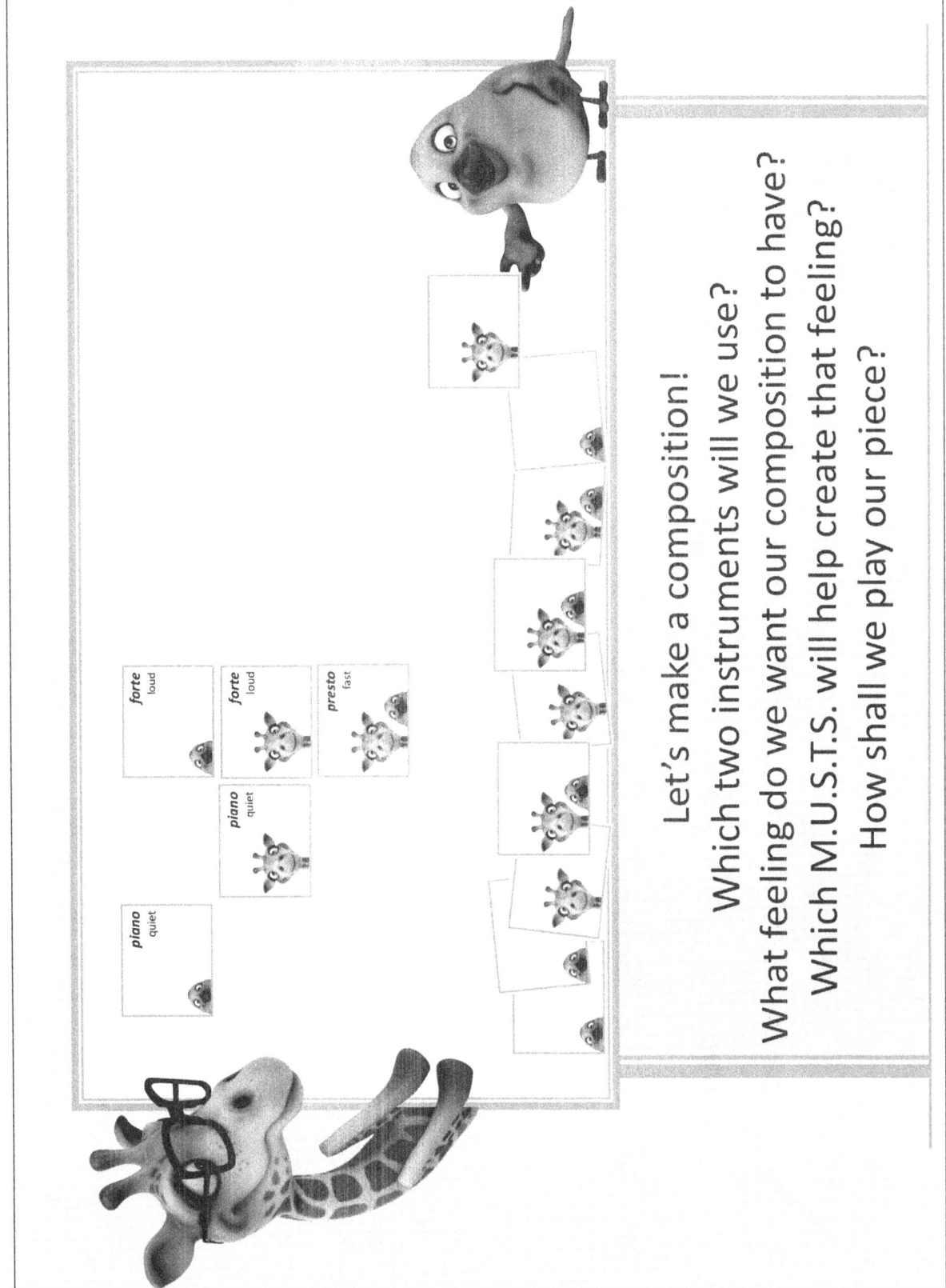

Source: Created by Michele Kaschub & Janice Smith with images from iStock/Credit: julos.

88 Chapter 15

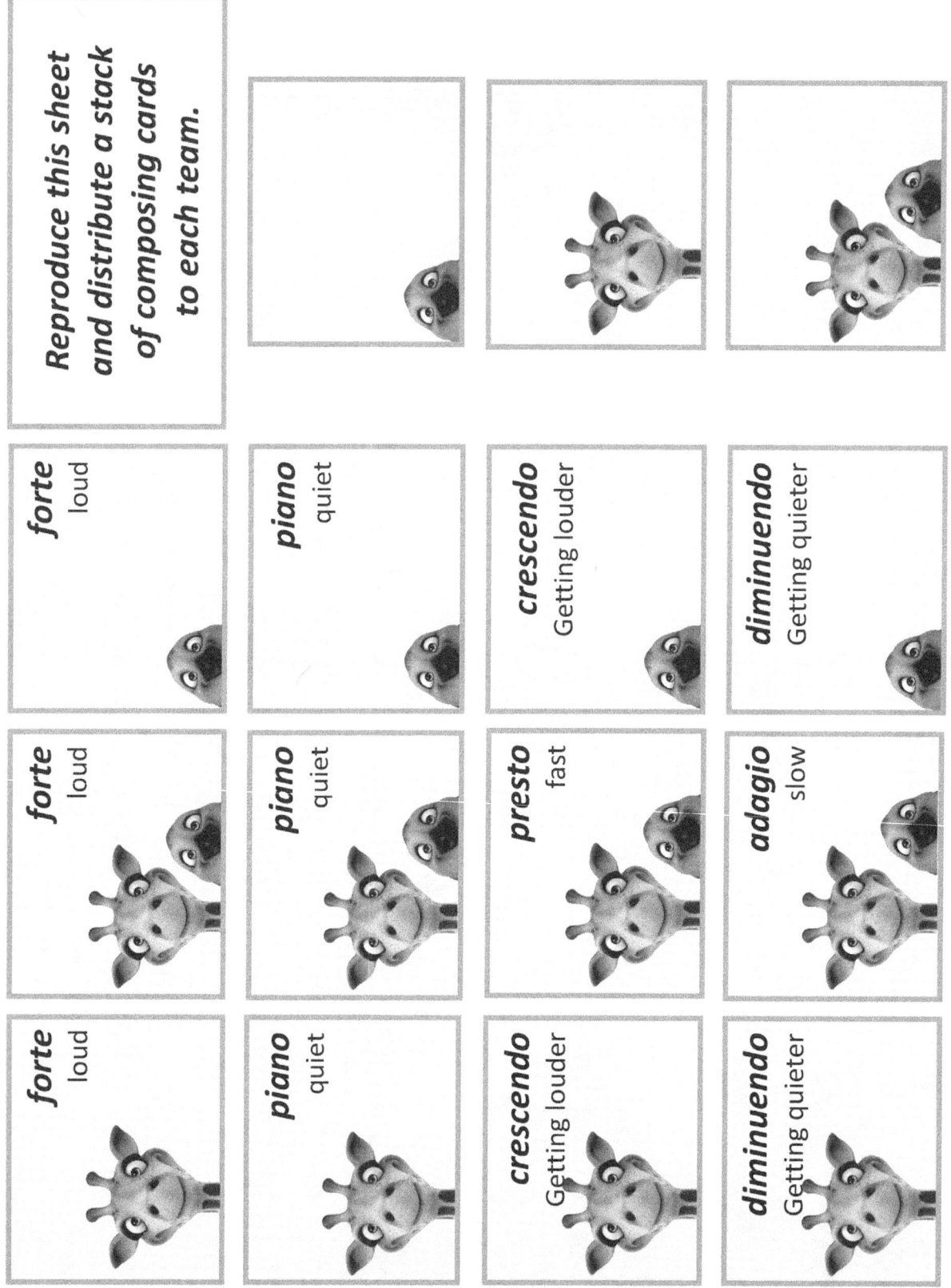

Source: Created by Michele Kaschub & Janice Smith with images from iStock/Credit: julos.

Chapter 16

Sound Blocks and Patterns

Electronic Music and Digital Media

About This Project

This project requires the use of software and tablets or similar devices to create pieces that emphasize musical form. Students use the *Sketchpages* to consider what kind of piece they wish to create and ideas of beginning, middle, and ending. They use the devices to select the sounds they will use and their plans to create the actual pieces. This activity can also be done acoustically, but it will have less variety and flexibility than it will if it is done with electronic media. It can be done as individual work or with a partner.

National Arts Standards for Music: Creating

This lesson presents students with an opportunity to:

Imagine
- MU:Cr1.1.1a With limited guidance, create musical ideas (such as answering a musical question) for a specific purpose.
- MU:Cr1.1b With limited guidance, generate musical ideas in multiple tonalities (such as major and minor) and meters (such as duple and triple).

Plan and Make
- MU:Cr2.1.1a With limited guidance, demonstrate and discuss personal reasons for selecting musical ideas that represent expressive intent.
- MU:Cr2.1.1b With limited guidance, use iconic or standard notation and/or recording technology to document and organize personal musical ideas.

Evaluate and Refine
- MU:Cr3.1.1a With limited guidance, discuss and apply personal, peer, and teacher feedback to refine personal musical ideas.

Present
- MU:Cr3.2.1a With limited guidance, convey expressive intent for a specific purpose by presenting a final version of personal musical ideas to peers or informal audience.

Materials

- *Sketchpages* for each composer or team of composers
- Optional compositional technique blocks *Sketchpage* from the Paired Composition lesson.

- Tools
  - Tablets or computers
  - Software such as *Tonepad*, *Pitch Painter*, *MusicLab*, *Groovy Music*, *Soundtrap*, and so on. The software used is not as important as its dependable availability and ease of use for the composers. Teachers need to be very familiar with whatever program they choose and prepared to troubleshoot. For simplicity, use only one software program at a time. Headphones are very desirable.

Project Time

- It will take approximately forty-five minutes to complete the lesson once the children are familiar with the software.

DISCUSSION QUESTIONS TO DEVELOP COMPOSITIONAL CAPACITIES

? Feelingful Intention—What kind of piece do you want to create? What will it make us feel when we hear it?
? Musical Expressivity—What kind of sounds will be used to invite that feeling? Will it be fast or slow, loud or quiet, and so on?
? Artistic Craftsmanship—Which sounds will you use? Make a plan for your piece, then create it. Listen to it and see if it sounds like you imagined it.

SEQUENCE OF ACTIVITIES

Before the composition activity can begin, the teacher needs to model what the software can do and how it works. The students then need some time to explore how the app/instrument works so that they can become familiar with its sound and capabilities. One way of modeling how to use the device and app might be to lead whole class projects like the ones in this book where students create music for scenes from a favorite picture book, or while building accompaniments for songs or other music making activities but do so while this software.

Another possibility is for teachers to help students create and save repeated patterns and then have students manipulate them in ways that emphasize unity and variety. Similarly, have the students create the same sounds, similar sounds, and different sounds using the selected software. Be sure the students understand and demonstrate how to save their work.

- Use the *Sketchpage* to introduce the project to the children. Have them think about the kind of piece they want to create: offer suggestions such as exciting, scary, silly, sad, sleepy, quiet, and so on. (Imagine)
- Using the *Sketchpage* and their chosen sounds, have the very young composers think about how they want their pieces to sound. Teachers may need to write vocabulary words on the board for students to write on their sketch pages or point to the word on a word wall. (Imagine)
- The very young composers then need to imagine how that music might sound and plan how the sounds work together. This plan does not have to be detailed and can be done after determining the sounds. (Imagine and Plan)
- Depending on the software, they will either create and save two or more sounds (more challenging) or choose two or more blocks of sounds from those available (easier).

** This step can also be done first. Very young composers can select sounds they like and then think about what kind of piece they want to make. Some very young composers find this simpler.

- Once they have their sounds selected, the very young composers should create a plan for how their sounds will fit together in their pieces. They draw the plan (score) on the *Sketchpage* and then play the piece from their score. The optional compositional technique blocks *Sketchpage* can be used for students who need ideas.

Usually, displaying those ideas somewhere in the classroom is enough to start them thinking about how things will fit together. (Plan and Make)
- Once the pieces are completed and have been practiced a bit, share them with the class and ask the very young composer to talk about what they were trying to create. Help the class discuss how successful that was. Ask if using the technology was helpful? Did they like using the program to create their pieces? Was it easier or harder? Why was that? (Present, Evaluate)

Optional Extensions

- Ask the very young composers what they think their next pieces might be like if they used the software again? Repeat the activity.
- Almost any of the lessons in this book can be adapted to use with software, but the instrumental music ones and the visual media ones often work the best.
- Make the very young composers' pieces available for them to share with their parents. Send a note to parents about what software was used and a few simple guidelines for helping their very young composer use it.

Source: Created by Michele Kaschub & Janice Smith with images from iStock/Credit: julos.

Chapter 17

Making A "When I Grow Up, I Want to Be" Song
Music Theater

About This Project

This project cultivates a child's ability to imagine what it is like to be grown up and have a job. It uses the child's ideas of what that job might be to explore what people who have that job do, and then uses that information and the reasons the job appeals to the child as a focal point for a song. This project is an individual one where each child works on his or her own piece. Teachers can model the process by talking about why they became teachers and what they like about their careers. The whole class can then make up a song about teaching to help children understand the steps for creating their own songs.

This project can be enhanced through collaboration with parents or community members with musical training or college students who need to spend time working with children in school classrooms. Helpers will need a few tips on how to guide young children to create a song without taking over the process, but then they can be useful assistants.

National Arts Standards: Creating

This lesson presents students with an opportunity to:

Imagine
- MU:Cr1.1.1a With limited guidance, create musical ideas (such as answering a musical question) for a specific purpose.
- MU:Cr1.1b With limited guidance, generate musical ideas in multiple tonalities (such as major and minor) and meters (such as duple and triple).

Plan and Make
- MU:Cr2.1.1a With limited guidance, demonstrate and discuss personal reasons for selecting musical ideas that represent expressive intent.
- MU:Cr2.1.1b With limited guidance, use iconic or standard notation and/or recording technology to document and organize personal musical ideas.

Evaluate and Refine
- MU:Cr3.1.1a With limited guidance, discuss and apply personal, peer, and teacher feedback to refine personal musical ideas.

Present
- MU:Cr3.2.1a With limited guidance, convey expressive intent for a specific purpose by presenting a final version of personal musical ideas to peers or informal audience.

Materials

- *Sketchpages*
- Second *Sketchpage* with partial lyrics, if used.
- Voices, recording devices, and possibly keyboard instruments

Project Time

- Discussion and modeling for this activity will take fifteen minutes.
- It will take approximately ten to fifteen minutes for students to create their songs once the background information has been created.
- Song sharing will take additional time.

DISCUSSION QUESTIONS TO DEVELOP COMPOSITIONAL CAPACITIES

? Feelingful Intention—What does it feel like to do this job? Does it change as the person goes through his or her day? Is it different at different times of the year?
? Musical Expressivity—How could that feeling sound? What kind of song will yours be?
? Artistic Craftsmanship—How many sections will your song have? (relates to whether the feeling changes.)

SEQUENCE OF ACTIVITIES

- This project works well if the classroom teachers are doing a focus on careers, but it also can be a standalone project. First, lead a discussion with the children about what they want to be when they grow up. Make a list and try to invite a variety of answers, that is, firefighters can be very popular! If one career is overpopulated, differentiate by location, that is, firefighters in cities, on ships, in forests, and so on (Imagine).
- Once a list has been made, talk about your own career choices and what you like about it. Share a list of several ideas: love working with children, get to perform every day for a live audience, have fun doing creative projects, enjoy seeing people learn new things, and so on. Then talk about how it feels to be a teacher. Emphasize the positive aspects.
- Use these to create song lyrics about being a teacher. You can have this all ready to use.

  Have the class help you create a song about being a teacher or share a song you have already made up about being a teacher that relates to the discussion you had with them about why you like being a teacher (Plan and Make). Here are some simple lyrics if you need them.

> The best music teacher
> Is what I want to be.
> I love to sing and play guitar
> And have you sing with me.
>
> I love it when we're having fun,
> I love the way we share
> I often see you working hard
> I hope you know I care.
>
> All year long I watch you grow,
> And teach you many things.
> It's such a joy to be with you.
> My heart just always sings.

- Have the children draw a picture on the *Sketchpage* of what they want to be and answer the questions about the job (Plan and Make). They may have to do some research to find out more about the job, and this could include talking to someone who does it. Parents and classroom teachers could facilitate this.
- Turn what they have learned about what is it like to do that job into a song using the second *Sketchpage* or have the children create their own (Plan and Make).

I want to be a _____ (name of job)
I think it would be fun.
I would _____ and _____ and _____ and _____. (things people do)
Until the day was done.
A _____, a _____ a _____ a _____ (repeat name of job)
Is what I want to be
A _____ and _____ (adjectives) _____ (name of job)
Is what I want to be.

Two examples:

    I want to be a firefighter
    I think it would be fun.
    I would drive the trucks and run the hose
    Until the day was done.

    A firefighter, a firefighter
    Is what I want to be
    A brave and strong firefighter
    Is what I want to be.

    I want to be a school nurse
    I think it would be fun.
    I would check your eyes and weight and height
    Until the day was done.

    A nurse, a nurse, a nurse, a nurse
    Is what I want to be.
    A kind and caring school nurse
    Is what I want to be.

    I want to be a school nurse
    I think it would be fun.
    I'd clean up scrapes and give out band-aids
    Until the day was done.

    A nurse, a nurse, a nurse, a nurse (repeat name of job)
    Is what I want to be
    A kind and caring school nurse
    Is what I want to be.

- Once the lyrics are written, talk with the child about the kind of feeling the song should have and encourage them to chant the words to help come up with a tune. Talk about whether the music might go upward or downward or stay the same and draw the shapes above the lyrics (Plan and Make).
- Encourage the child to sing a tune to the words, maybe starting with the chorus first and record what they do. Help them shape it into a song to share (Evaluate and Refine).

- Notate the child's piece for them and give them a copy. This can be done at the next class or put on a website with the recording for parents to see and hear (Present).

Optional Extensions

This project obviously requires many helpful musicians in order to do it with each child, but there are several options for music teachers without volunteers to use when doing this lesson. One option is simply to choose a career and write a song about that with the whole class. Another option is to have the children do the picture and description and then work with a few each class to have them make up a tune and record it. A third possibility is that the children do the *Sketchpage* for the song, and the whole class makes up the tune. This works especially well for shy or unwilling singers.

Source: Created by Michele Kaschub & Janice Smith with images from iStock/Credit: julos.

LYRIC TEMPLATE 1

I want to be a _____,
                  (name of job)

I think it would be fun!

I would _____, and _____,
        (things people do)

and _____,

Until the day was done!

LYRIC TEMPLATE 2

A _____, a _____,
                    (repeat name of job)

a _____,

Is what I want to be.

A _____ and _____
  (adjective)   (adjective)

_____,
(name of job)

Is what I want to be!

Source: Created by Michele Kaschub & Janice Smith.

PROJECTS FOR GRADE 2

Chapter 18

A Song for Grandparents' Day
Songwriting

About This Project

Sometimes very young composers want to honor someone in their lives. A "Song for Grandparents' Day" can be used as a whole class project, or class project with individually composed verses. Advanced very young composers can create their own songs, particularly if they have already had numerous songwriting experiences.

National Arts Standards for Music: Creating

This lesson presents students with an opportunity to:

Imagine
- MU:Cr1.1.2a Improvise rhythmic and melodic patterns and musical ideas for a specific purpose.
- MU:Cr1.1.2b Generate musical patterns and ideas within the context of a given tonality (such as major and minor) and meter (such as duple and triple).

Plan and Make
- MU:Cr2.1.2a Demonstrate and explain personal reasons for selecting patterns and ideas for music that represent expressive intent.
- MU:Cr2.1.2b Use iconic or standard notation and/or recording technology to combine, sequence, and document personal musical ideas.

Evaluate and Refine
- MU:Cr3.1.2a Interpret and apply personal, peer, and teacher feedback to revise personal music.

Present
- MU:Cr3.2.2a Convey expressive intent or a specific purpose by presenting a final version of personal musical ideas to peers or informal audience.

Materials
- *Sketchpages*
- Tools: voices, recording device

Project Time

- It will take approximately 30 minutes to do this activity as a whole class project. It works well to use ten minutes of class time over each of several days. There are indications in the Sequence of Activities for how to divide these activities over four class meetings.

DISCUSSION QUESTIONS TO DEVELOP COMPOSITIONAL CAPACITIES

? Feelingful Intention—How would you describe your grandmother or grandfather? (pick one? Or write about both?) How do you feel when you are with them?
? Musical Expressivity—How would you create music that feels like being with grandparent? Would it have lots of motion or stasis? Unity or variety? Sound or silence? Tension? Would it be stable or have unexpected sounds?
? Artistic Craftsmanship—What compositional tools will we use to make our grandparents' song(s)?

SEQUENCE OF ACTIVITIES

- Create the words for the song. Brainstorm words that describe grandparents in general and how the children feel about them. You may also want to include things that the children like to do with their grandparents. (Imagine)
- Using words that they came up frequently, help the children create the chorus for the song. (Plan and Make) If possible, these should rhyme and be easy to sing. For example (in compound duple meter):

    Grandparents are wonderful people
    That sometimes live far away.
    They talk and read and play with us
    We love when they come to stay.

- Create the text for the verse or verses in a similar manner. This can be done on a separate day. If this is a whole class project, you may want to create the words for the verses and have the very young composers create the music. However, it is often more satisfying (but more time consuming) to help the class to this. One or two verses is usually plenty. One way to do this is one verse about grandmothers and another about grandfathers. You can also decide this after the tunes are made up. (Plan and Make)
- Have the children decide whether to begin with the verse or the chorus. Make up the tune using the same sort of processes described in the other songwriting lessons in other parts of this book. See Teddy Bear Lullabies (p. 51) and Field Trip Song (p. 77). (Plan and Make) These ideas include:
- Talk with the class about how the tune should go: upward, downward, stay the same; draw lines over the words in the shapes they suggest (Plan and Make).
  ○ ask for volunteers to sing their ideas for the first line, then sing them back to the class and have the whole class echo the idea; jot the idea down quickly in notation as well as record it. After hearing several ideas, ask which one seems to fit the line best. Make a decision, and move on to the next line. Revise ideas as necessary. (Evaluate and Refine)
  ○ OR have the class sing their ideas all at once and listen for an idea that you sing to the class. Follow the procedure above. (Plan and Make; Evaluate and Refine)
  ○ OR if you have xylophones or keyboards, have the class chant the words and make up a tune that fits them as they chant. Remind the class that they must be able to sing what they make up. Hint: big leaps are not easy to sing. (Plan and Make; Evaluate and Refine)

- When this part is finished, notate it and go on to something else for the rest of the class.
  - In the next class, make up a tune for the other part of the song using the same or similar processes.
  - Notate the whole song in a format that can be shared with the class. (Plan and Make; Evaluate and Refine)
- Consider adding instruments to the song. Have the children make suggestions and try out their ideas. (Plan and Make; Evaluate and Refine)
- Rehearse the song and plan for a performance. (Present)
- After the performance, ask the class to describe for the audience how they made up the song. Once the discussion is over, perform the piece again and make a recording to share on the class website. (Present)

Optional Extension

This project can be used to write about any person in the very young composer's life. It works equally well for Mother's Day, Father's Day, or visiting relatives from away. It can also be adapted to use with "best friends" or a child who is moving to a new school.

Source: Created by Michele Kaschub & Janice Smith with images from iStock/Credit: julos, tomap49, and Allevinatis.

Chapter 19

Exploring Leitmotif: The Mitten
Composition and Visual Media

About This Project

This lesson uses a picture book that tells a cumulative story to introduce the idea of *leitmotif* in music writing. Cumulative tales add characters with each new story event and these characters remain part of the narrative until its very end. This lesson is based on *The Mitten* by Jan Brett (Putnam, 1989). Additional story options are listed at the end of this lesson. For each character in the story, a *leitmotif* is created and used to accompany a reading of the story. This project is similar to the *Gingerbread Man* lesson on p. 55 except that the students are challenged to think more deeply about the expressive qualities of the character and how these qualities relate to the other characters and their *leitmotivs*. The lesson works well with students working in pairs and small groups, but it could also be structured as a whole class activity.

National Arts Standards for Music: Creating

This lesson presents students with an opportunity to:

Imagine
- MU:Cr1.1.2a Improvise rhythmic and melodic patterns and musical ideas for a specific purpose.
- MU:Cr1.1.2b Generate musical patterns and ideas within the context of a given tonality (such as major and minor) and meter (such as duple and triple).

Plan and Make
- MU:Cr2.1.2a Demonstrate and explain personal reasons for selecting patterns and ideas for music that represent expressive intent.
- MU:Cr2.1.2b Use iconic or standard notation and/or recording technology to combine, sequence, and document personal musical ideas.

Evaluate and Refine
- MU:Cr3.1.2a Interpret and apply personal, peer, and teacher feedback to revise personal music.

Present
- MU:Cr3.2.2a Convey expressive intent or a specific purpose by presenting a final version of personal musical ideas to peers or informal audience.

Materials
- *Sketchpages*

- Tools: a variety of sound sources; can be done with just voices, or with instruments, or with electronic sound sources.

Project Time

- It will take approximately five minutes per character once the process is understood; one forty-minute class for the whole project if done as a whole class project

DISCUSSION QUESTIONS TO DEVELOP COMPOSITIONAL CAPACITIES

? Feelingful Intention—How does this character differ from all the others in the story? What feelings does the character have? How does the character feel similar to the others? How do the others feel about this character?
? Musical Expressivity—How would you describe the music that represents this character? (Use the MUSTS)
? Artistic Craftsmanship—What sounds shall we use to make the character sound like that?

SEQUENCE OF ACTIVITIES

- Present the idea of creating a special theme for each character in a story book that you are about to read. Ask the children to pick a character that they like and think about how it would feel to be that character (Imagine). Read the story and then discuss their impressions.
- Introduce the term *leitmotif* and explain that it is shorter than a whole song or even a theme but that it is associated with a particular character or feeling in a story. With the class, make a list of the characters and events in the story that the students believe should have their own *leitmotif* (Plan and Make). Keep the list shorter for a whole class activity; make it much longer if the class will work in pairs or individually.
- Model a discussion with the whole class of two of the items from the list or work through the entire story that way. With some classes, it is possible to have them work in pairs or individually to come up with a *leitmotif* for one of the items on the list (Plan and Make).
  ○ For example, ask if the children have noticed that Nicki is on each page—but that he seems unaware of what is going on with the mitten. How should his music feel? Does it change at any point? Do the animals notice ever notice him? Should his music blend in with the other characters or contrast with them? How shall we make that happen?
  ○ Use the *Sketchpage* to record their decisions. Then make up music for Nicki. If the decision is that it should blend in with the other leitmotivs, you may want to encourage Nicki's music to be somewhat repetitive and simple so that the other animals can more easily fit with it.
  ○ Ask for student ideas using whatever sounds are available: instruments, voices, and so on encourage a "walking" feeling and perhaps use a longer version near the beginning of the book but shorter parts of the idea later in the book.
- Next, decide whether the mitten itself needs a *leitmotif* and, if so, create that in a similar way (Plan and Make).
- Move on to the first animal—the mole: ask what the children know about moles and help them describe how the mole might feel and how the music should sound (Imagine). Have several students offer ideas for mole music and help the class decide which one "fits" the idea of the mole the best (Plan and Make). Then determine how it fits with Nicki's music or if the two musical ideas should remain separate from each other (Plan and Make).
- Go on to the next animal: the rabbit. How is the rabbit different from the mole? Is there anything similar about them? How should the music for the rabbit sound (Imagine)? How will it fit with the music for the mole? Does it happen at the same time or before or after the mole music (Plan and Make)?
- At this point, the class can continue through the book the same way or separate to work on individual characters on their own using the *Sketchpage* as a guide (Plan and Make).

- Once all the *leitmotivs* are ready, perform the story using the additional sounds, record the performance, and listen to it. Ask which parts were most effective with the story. Is there anything that needs to be changed (Evaluate and Refine)? Work through any needed revisions, then record again and share with other classes and with parents on a class website (Present).

Optional Extension

Days of the week books such as Eric Carle's *Today Is Monday* (Puffin Books, 1993) can also be used, and *leitmotivs* can be lengthened into themes for each day.

A FEW CUMULATIVE BOOKS

The Great Big Enormous Turnip by Aleksey Tolstoy and Helen Oxenbury (Macmillan, 1972)
The Napping House by Audrey Wood and Don Wood (Harcourt Brace Jovanovich, 1984)
This Is The House that Jack Built by many illustrators including Mandy Patinkin (Puffin Books, 2004)
The House that Drac Built by Judy Sierra and Will Hillenbrand (Collier Books, 1995)
Whopper Cake by Karma Wilson and Will Hillenbrand (McElderry Books, 2006)
The Little Old Lady Who Was Not Afraid of Anything by Linda Williams and Cecelia DeWolf (Harper Collins, 1986)

There are many others. Look for holiday stories, counting books and days of the week books. Children's librarians can be a valuable resource for these kinds of stories. Avoid those stories that already have a well-known melody such as *I Know An Old Lady Who Swallowed a Fly* and *The Twelve Days of Christmas*, as this may make the process of creating original music much more challenging.

Source: Created by Michele Kaschub & Janice Smith with images from iStock/Credit: julos, Maksym Chechel, and Aim Yusifov.

Chapter 20

Chamber Music Trios
Instrumental Music

About This Project

In this activity students will create instrumental compositions using three contrasting sounds in a variety of combinations. Each group will have one pitched and two unpitched instruments. This project can also be done with other configurations of pitched and unpitched instruments, but the use of multiple pitched instruments will work best if a pentatonic scale is used. Composers will select a feeling, choose instruments, and create a performance plan (who will play, what will they play, and when will they play it). They work together to make the parts fit with one another and rehearse their pieces for a class performance.

National Arts Standards for Music: Creating

This lesson presents students with an opportunity to:

Imagine
- MU:Cr1.1.2a Improvise rhythmic and melodic patterns and musical ideas for a specific purpose.
- MU:Cr1.1.2b Generate musical patterns and ideas within the context of a given tonality (such as major and minor) and meter (such as duple and triple).

Plan and Make
- MU:Cr2.1.2a Demonstrate and explain personal reasons for selecting patterns and ideas for music that represent expressive intent.
- MU:Cr2.1.2b Use iconic or standard notation and/or recording technology to combine, sequence, and document personal musical ideas.

Evaluate and Refine
- MU:Cr3.1.2a Interpret and apply personal, peer, and teacher feedback to revise personal music.

Present
- MU:Cr3.2.2a Convey expressive intent or a specific purpose by presenting a final version of personal musical ideas to peers or informal audience.

Materials

- *Sketchpages*
- A variety of pitched and unpitched percussion instruments preset into similar-sounding groups: wooden ones, drums, metal ones, and pitched keyboards.

Project Time

- It will take approximately twenty minutes to do the entire lesson, longer if the book is read to the class as a first step.

DISCUSSION QUESTIONS TO DEVELOP COMPOSITIONAL CAPACITIES

? Feelingful Intention—What will be the mood of our piece?
? Musical Expressivity—What kinds of sounds do we want people to experience so that they will understand the feeling of our piece?
? Artistic Craftsmanship—How will we create our piece with the instruments we have chosen?

SEQUENCE OF ACTIVITIES

- Consider reading the book *Max Found Two Sticks* by Brian Pinkney (Aladdin, 1997) and lead a discussion about how Max expresses himself without using words. Talk about music that has no words and uses only instruments (Imagine).
- Play a few short examples of instrumental chamber music, including a percussion ensemble piece. Ask the children to describe the feeling each excerpt suggests. Point out that not all the instruments play all the time, but also take turns and play in small groups.
- Use the *Sketchpage* to explain the task. The teacher can model doing this, but the activity is designed for groups of three. Each group decides on what kind of piece they want to create (Imagine). A word wall of feeling words such as silly, scared, happy, sad, angry, excited, proud, and so on, can be helpful in case the children need ideas.
- Explain that when it is time to choose instruments, the children should select only one from each group so that each sound will be clearly heard and not covered up by the other sounds. Explain and discuss contrasting timbres. Remind the children that everyone in each group needs to have something to play (Plan and Make).
- One of the challenges of this activity is getting three students to play at the same time and at the same speed (Present). They may need to practice this a bit. They also need to figure out how to start and how to end. Encourage them to decide this as they work and give several examples of how this can be done (one person starts, and the others join in; someone counts off and everyone starts; they take a breath and nod, etc.).
- The children use their *Sketchpages* to plan their pieces, then share the plan with their teacher. Then they select instruments and work out their pieces (Plan and Make). Does their plan work? Do they need to change anything (Evaluate and Refine)? Practice a few more times until the performance goes smoothly, then perform for each other (Present).

Optional Extension

- This project can also be done with electronic instruments producing the sounds.
- The quality of the pieces often improves when this activity is repeated at different points during the year.
- Structure the activity to purposefully explore different musical elements and compositional techniques. For example, how might students make use of an ostinato or explore the implications of changing dynamics?

Source: Created by Michele Kaschub & Janice Smith with images from iStock/Credit: julos, Inna Kharlamova, and vladars.

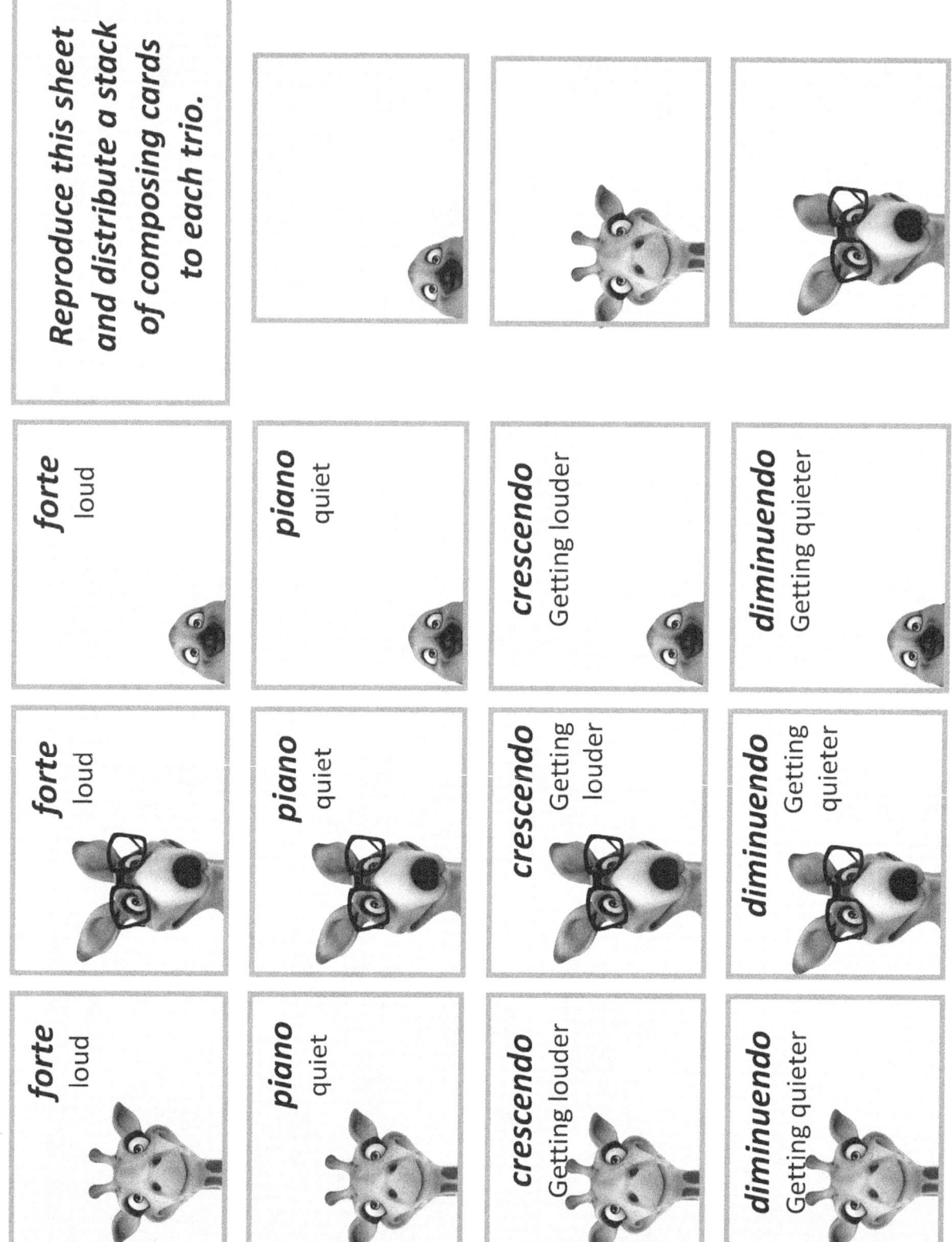

Source: Created by Michele Kaschub & Janice Smith with images from iStock/Credit: julos.

Chamber Music Trios 113

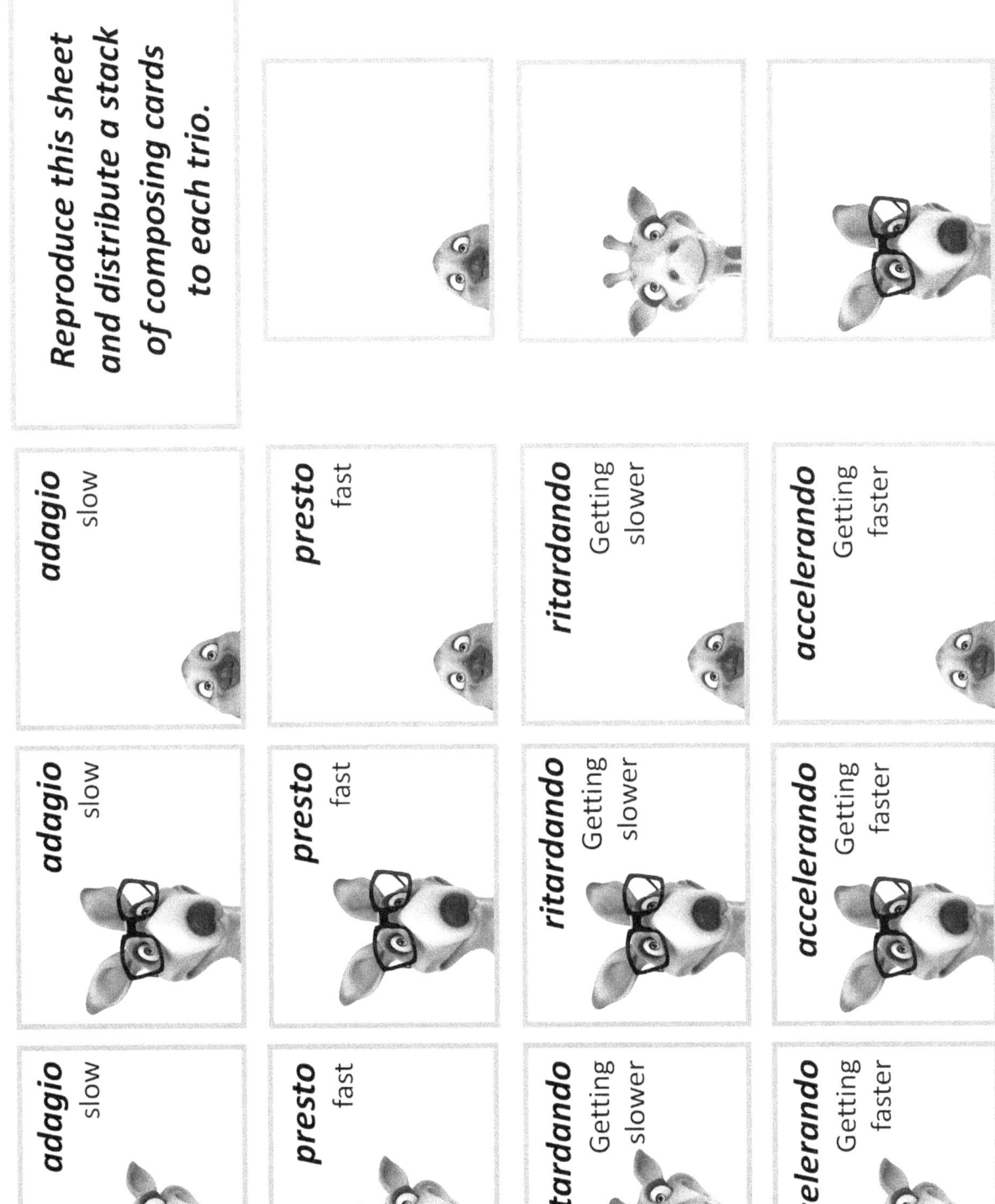

Source: Created by Michele Kaschub & Janice Smith with images from iStock/Credit: julos.

Chapter 21

Terrific Textures

Electronic Music and Digital Media

About This Project

This project requires the use of software and tablets or similar devices to create pieces that feature layers of sound. Students use the *Sketchpages* to consider what kind of piece they wish to create and to sketch their ideas of when sounds play together and when they occur separately. They use the devices to select the sounds they will use to make the pieces. This activity can also be done acoustically, but it will have less variety and flexibility than it will if it is done with electronic media. It can be done as individual work or with a partner or even with several children working together.

National Arts Standards for Music: Creating

This lesson presents students with an opportunity to:

Imagine
- MU:Cr1.1.2a Improvise rhythmic and melodic patterns and musical ideas for a specific purpose.
- MU:Cr1.1.2b Generate musical patterns and ideas within the context of a given tonality (such as major and minor) and meter (such as duple and triple).

Plan and Make
- MU:Cr2.1.2a Demonstrate and explain personal reasons for selecting patterns and ideas for music that represent expressive intent.
- MU:Cr2.1.2b Use iconic or standard notation and/or recording technology to combine, sequence, and document personal musical ideas.

Evaluate and Refine
- MU:Cr3.1.2a Interpret and apply personal, peer, and teacher feedback to revise personal music.

Present

- MU:Cr3.2.2a Convey expressive intent or a specific purpose by presenting a final version of personal musical ideas to peers or informal audience.

Materials
- *Sketchpages*
- Tablets or computers

- Software such as *Tonepad*, *Pitch Painter*, *MusicLab*, *Groovy Music*, *Soundtrap*, and so on. The software used is not as important as its dependable availability and ease of use for the composers. Teachers need to be very familiar with whatever program they choose and prepared to troubleshoot. For simplicity, use only one software program at a time. Headphones are very desirable.

Project Time

- It will take approximately fifteen minutes to complete the lesson once the children are familiar with the software.

DISCUSSION QUESTIONS TO DEVELOP COMPOSITIONAL CAPACITIES

? Feelingful Intention—What sounds are you going to use? What feelings do they seem to have?
? Musical Expressivity—How do you imagine this music will sound?
? Artistic Craftsmanship—Which sounds will you use when? Will they play at the same time? One after the other?

SEQUENCE OF ACTIVITIES

- The teacher should model what the software can do and how it works so that the students become familiar with it. Doing whole class projects like the ones in this book, creating background music for scenes from a favorite picture book, or accompaniments for songs are all ways teachers can use the software creatively and model it for the students.
- For this lesson, model how layers of sound can fit together. Pay special attention to how the sounds vary in tone color and how sounds provide contrast of various kinds. The goal is to experiment with timbres and how they work in layers (loud sounds mask quiet ones, two sounds can hide each other, two sounds can combine into one blended sound, etc). Show how to create or audition sounds within the software and how to save their work.
- Use the *Sketchpage* to introduce the project to the children. Have them play with the sounds and find two or three that they think will fit together to make their piece (Plan and Make). Have them make an icon or drawing for each sound (like a key for a map). Then ask them to think about how their piece will go. Imagine or experiment with when the sounds will start and end, when they will play together and when they will play alone (Imagine). Draw a score using lines to show when each sound will play and when they will be silent (Plan and Make).
- Ask the children to play the piece from their score (Present). Did it sound like they imagined? Would they like to make any changes (Evaluate and Refine)? (Students may need additional copies of the *Sketchpage* to capture their thinking.) Encourage students to practice playing their pieces a few times and then perform their compositions for the class (Present).

Optional Extension

- Have the children play their maps on acoustic instruments. How did the character of the piece change?
- Have the children create a piece where the whole class is involved. Each child contributes one sound and creates a motif or pattern with their sound. Which sounds work well together? Which ones contrast? How might we create a piece that everyone plays? What would that feel like? How shall we start? What happens next? How shall we end?

Terrific Textures

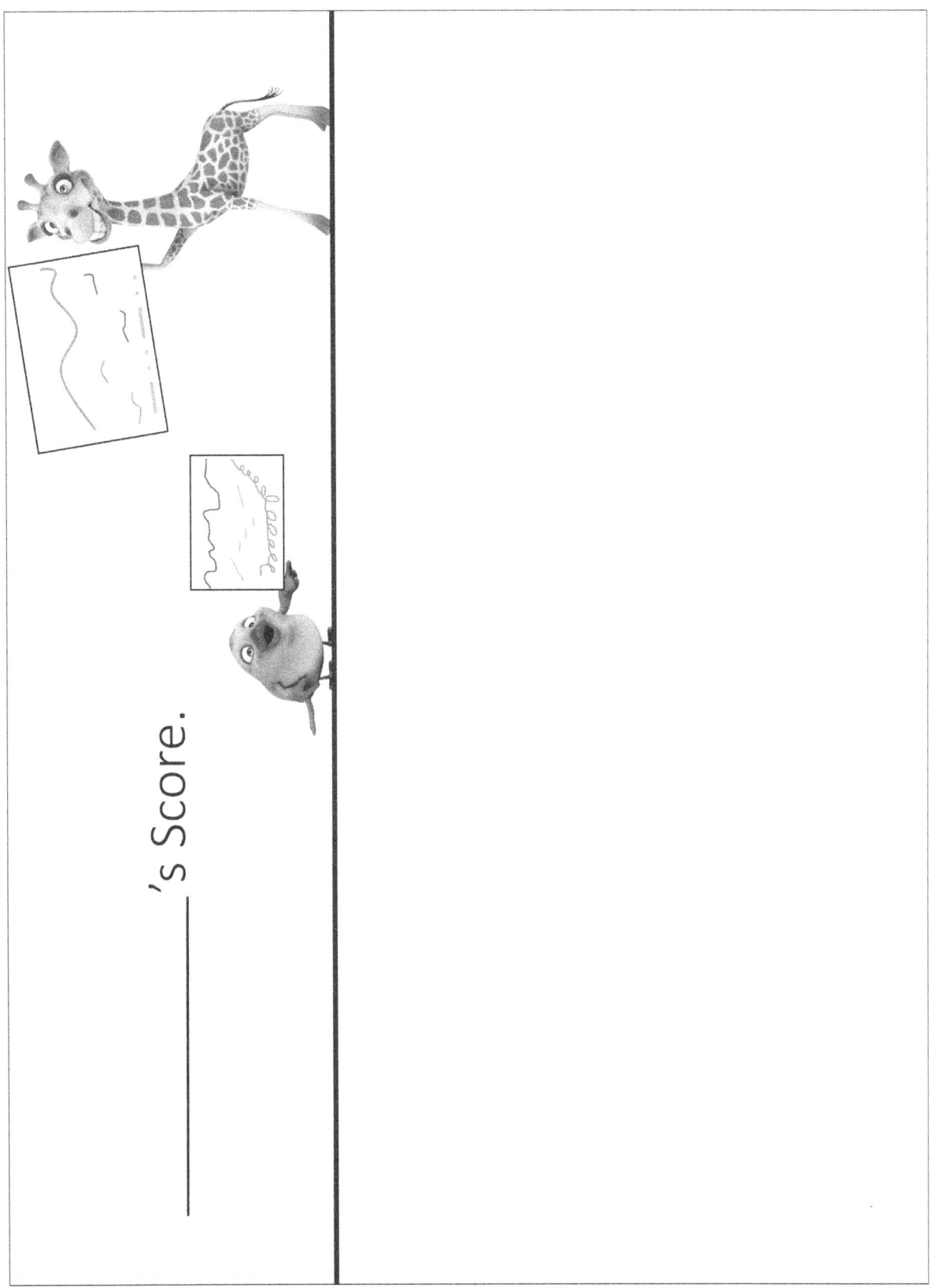

_____'s Score.

Source: Created by Michele Kaschub & Janice Smith with images from iStock/Credit: julos.

Chapter 22

Incidental Music for Puppet Theater
Music Theater

About This Project

Theater activities with very young children can be imaginative and engaging. Using puppet theater with very young composers combines literacy with musical and social skills, including cooperation, communication, and problem-solving. Anyone can participate and can play any role without being limited by age, gender, or ethnicity. For example, in telling the story of *The Three Little Pigs*, anyone can play any of the characters. In this activity, the children will create incidental music and sound effects to accompany a puppet theater production of a folktale for which the classroom has the puppets.

A more elaborate version would require the children to create their own story using whatever puppets are available. Students will be encouraged to create at least one song for a main character and music to start and end their performances. Background music can be added as needed. This project can be a whole class activity or done in groups after the teacher models the process.

National Arts Standards for Music: Creating

This lesson presents students with an opportunity to:

Imagine
- MU:Cr1.1.2a Improvise rhythmic and melodic patterns and musical ideas for a specific purpose.
- MU:Cr1.1.2b Generate musical patterns and ideas within the context of a given tonality (such as major and minor) and meter (such as duple and triple).

Plan and Make
- MU:Cr2.1.2a Demonstrate and explain personal reasons for selecting patterns and ideas for music that represent expressive intent.
- MU:Cr2.1.2b Use iconic or standard notation and/or recording technology to combine, sequence, and document personal musical ideas.

Evaluate and Refine
- MU:Cr3.1.2a Interpret and apply personal, peer, and teacher feedback to revise personal music.

Present
- MU:Cr3.2.2a Convey expressive intent or a specific purpose by presenting a final version of personal musical ideas to peers or informal audience.

Materials

- *Sketchpages*
- Puppets and a puppet stage.
- A variety of small percussion and other sound sources.

Project Time

- It will take approximately ninety minutes to complete this activity, preferably spread over several music classes and interspersed with other activities.

DISCUSSION QUESTIONS TO DEVELOP COMPOSITIONAL CAPACITIES

? Feelingful Intention—How do the characters feel?
? Musical Expressivity—How would music that feels that was sound? Which of the M.U.S.T. S. will be important for each character?
? Artistic Craftsmanship—When in the story will we use music? What instruments will we use? Who will play them? Will the musicians be hidden or visible?

SEQUENCE OF ACTIVITIES

Day 1

- Introduce the activity to the children either by selecting a favorite story to use or presenting a story you have chosen. Review the outlines of the story with the children so that the main ideas are fresh in their memories.
- Using the *In the beginning Sketchpage*, decide how the play will begin (Plan and Make). Talk about what kind of music might be playing before the curtain opens and during the first scene. Make notes on the *Sketchpage* about how the children think the music should sound Plan and Make).

Day 2

- Using the *Next* and *Then Sketchpages* use a similar process to plan the music for the rest of the play (Plan and Make). One of the scenes might need to have a song for a particular character in it. For example, *Little Red Riding Hood* might need a song to sing on the way to Grandma's house. In the *Three Billy Goats Gruff*, the troll might need a song. The person playing that character puppet can make up the song, or the class can write it for the character to sing (Plan and Make). If using the whole class to do this, do it next using the techniques described elsewhere in this book. (See Teddy Bear Lullabies, Field Trip Song, Grandparents Song.)
- Once the ideas have been collected on the *Sketchpages*, decide which children will be the performers, which will be the musicians, which will announce the play, which will turn the lights on and off, and who will do any other tasks that might be needed to put on a performance. Most of the class should wind up being musicians for the various scenes (Plan and Make).

Day 3

- Divide the musicians into groups by scene as described on the *Sketchpages* and have them create the music for the scenes (Plan and Make). Have the puppeteers practice their parts in the story without the music.
- When the musicians have finished their work, have them perform their pieces for the class (Present). Discuss whether any adjustments need to be made (Evaluate and Refine). Then run the play with the music (Present).

Day 4

- Next, discuss whether any other sound is needed. A knock on the door? Hoofbeats on a bridge? Etc. (Evaluate and Refine).
- Practice the play several times and film the performances (Present). Watch the film and suggest improvements (Evaluate and Refine).

Day 5

- Present it as a performance for another class or other audience (Present).

Optional Extensions

One extension is to have the children create their own stories. They can also make puppets of various kinds: Stick puppets, sock puppets, paper bag puppets, and so on.

A blanket over a piece of rope above a table covered with another blanket can function as a theater, as can a large box (refrigerator?) turned sideways on a table.

Using the book *Throw Your Tooth on the Roof: Tooth Traditions from Around the World* by Selby B. Beeler and illustrated by G. Brian Karas (Houghton Mifflin, 1998) have the children create stories about losing a tooth in another country. They will have to imagine what that might be like to live in that place, and what the child who loses the tooth might do to create a short story about it. This activity can be extended by talking about traditional folk music from those countries, how it sounds, and what makes it sound that way.

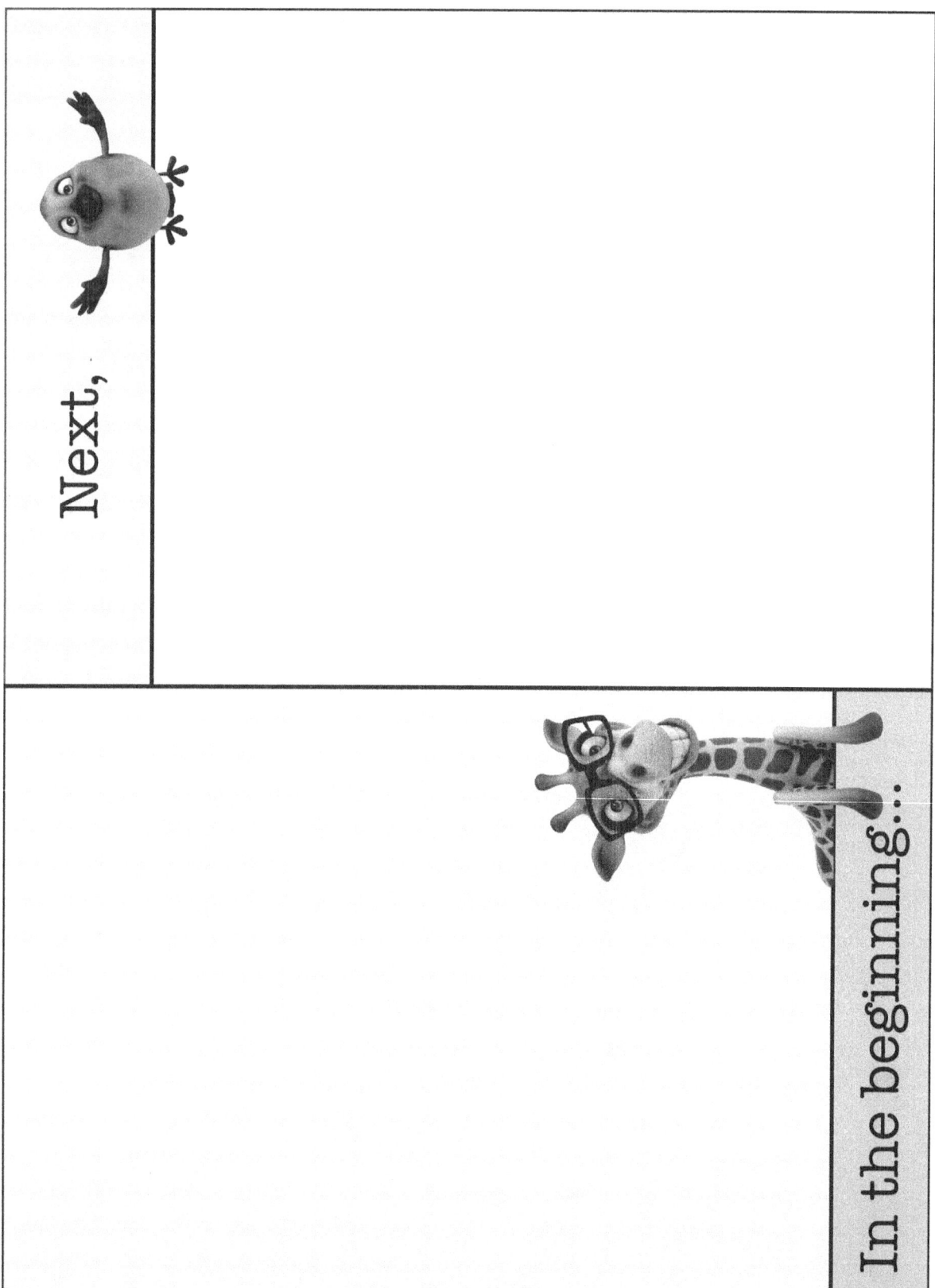

Source: Created by Michele Kaschub & Janice Smith with images from iStock/Credit: julos.

Incidental Music for Puppet Theater 123

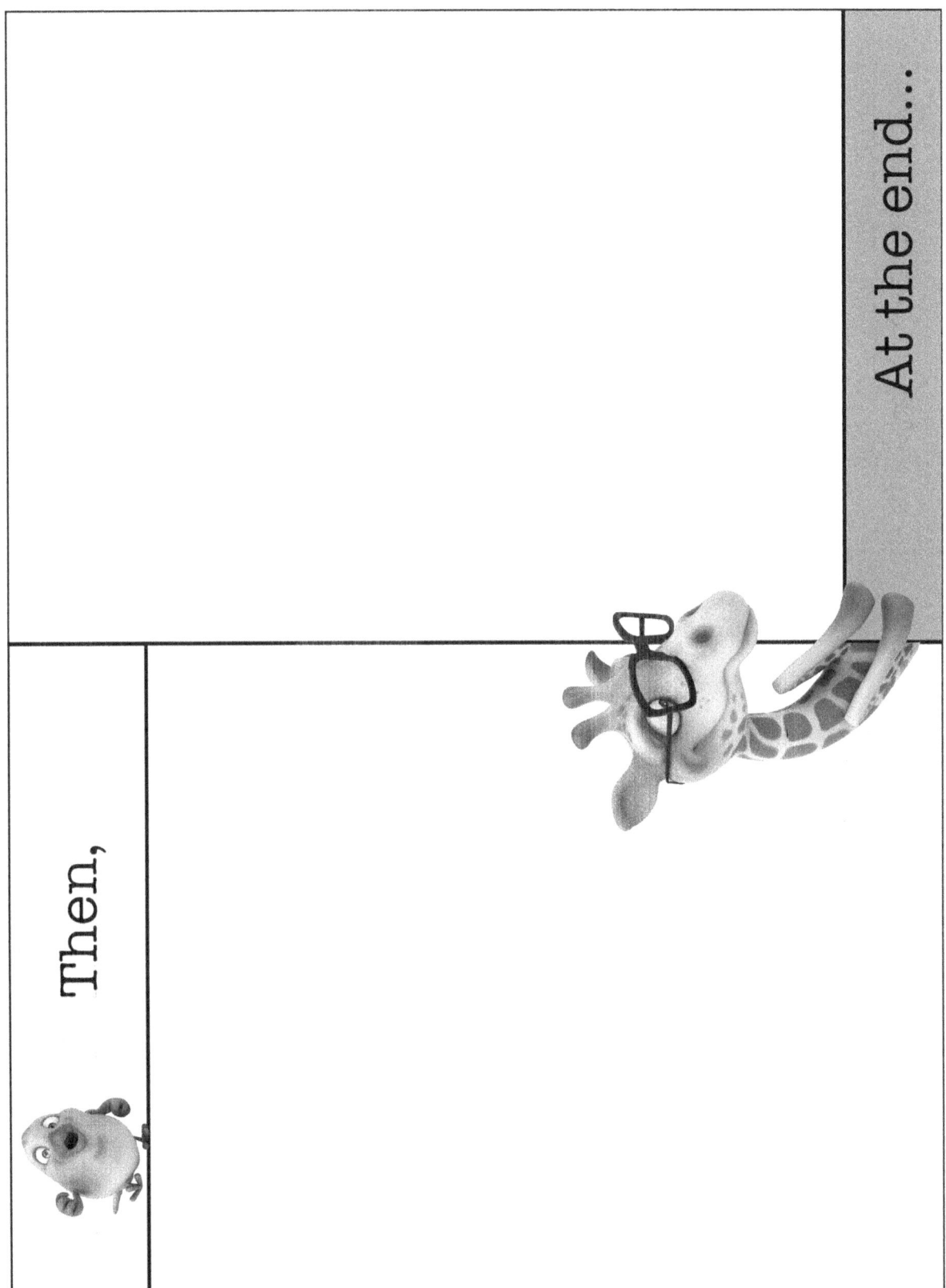

Source: Created by Michele Kaschub & Janice Smith with images from iStock/Credit: julos.

Appendix: Notation Templates

Title:
Composer(s):

for composers using invented or iconograhic notation

Source: Created by Michele Kaschub & Janice Smith.

Title:
Composer(s):

for composers using invented or iconograhic notation in partnership with traditional notation
(best for use as a memory booster before part alignment is desired)

Source: Created by Michele Kaschub & Janice Smith.

Appendix

Title:
Composer(s):

*for composers using invented or iconograhic notation in partnership with traditional notation
(best for use when part alignment is needed)*

Source: Created by Michele Kaschub & Janice Smith.

Title:
Composer(s):

for composers using traditional notation

Source: Created by Michele Kaschub & Janice Smith.

Index

Note: Page numbers given in *italics* denotes pages with Tables or Figures.

activities: individual, 11, 22, 30, 36, 55–57, 71, 89, 93–96, 106, 115; partnered, 21, 28, 30, 42, 85–86, 89, 115; small group, 3, 11, 27, 28, 30, 36, 40, 42, 43, 85–86, 105, 109–10, 119–21; whole class, 7, 15, 16, 21, 27, 28, 30, 36, 37, 39, 40, 42, 47, 48, 52, 55–57, 71–72, 77–78, 90, 93–96, 101–3, 105–7, 119–21
anchor charts, 38
aptitude, 15
articulation techniques, 25
artistic autonomy, 3, 4, 11, 33
artistic craftsmanship, 4, 15, 20–21, 25, 27, 29, 42, 43, 47, 52, 56, 64, 68, 78, 82, 86, 90, 94, 102, 106, 110, 116, 120
artistic purpose, 4, 16, 43
artistic thinking, 20
audience: experience of, 22, 30, 36, 43; perceptions of, 22; reactions of, 39, 41, 43, 77, 81, 85, 89, 93, 101, 105, 109, 115, 119

Beethoven, Ludwig von, 3
Bruner, Jerome, 35, 43n1

canon, 25, 48
Classic Children's Fairy tales: The Gingerbread Man, 55, 105
collaborative learning, 3
communication skills, 39
composer's circles, 3, 40–41
composer's sketchbook, 3, 27, 68
composer's voice, 3, 4
composers: characteristics of, 4, 9; peer interaction, 3, 9, 16, 39, 40, 42, 51, 55, 63, 67, 71, 77, 81, 85, 89, 93, 101, 105, 109, 115, 119; and reluctance to share work, 42
composing; for characters, 36–37, 48, 81–82, 105–7, 119–21; in digital media, 47, 48, 67–69, 89–91, 115–16; and electronic music, 3, 24, 47, 67–69, 89–91, 115–16; instrumental music, 3, 9, 10, 34, 47–48, 63–64, 85–85, 91, 109–10; for music theater, 3, 47–48, 71–72, 93–96, 119–21; and songwriting, 34–36, 47–48, 51–52, 77–78, 101–3; and visual media, 47–48, 55–57, 81–82, 105–7
compositional capacities, 11, 15–25, 27–29, 37, 39, 42, 47, 52, 55, 56, 64, 68, 72, 78, 82, 86, 90, 94, 102, 106, 110, 116, 120
compositional task, 3, 19, 28, 33–36
compositional working groupings: with a partner, 3, 21, 28, 30, 42, 85–86, 89–91, 105, 115–17; in a small group, 3, 11, 15, 28, 30, 36, 105–7, 109–10, 119; as a whole class, 15, 16, 27, 36, 37, 39, 40, 42, 47, 48, 52, 55, 56, 71, 72, 77, 78, 90, 93, 96, 101, 102, 105, 106, 116, 119, 120; working alone, 20, 28, 36, 42, 89–91, 115–17
compositions; providing feedback about, 3, 11, 29, 33, 39–42, 51, 55, 63, 67, 71, 77, 81, 85, 89, 93, 101, 105, 109, 115, 119; sharing, 3–4, 11, 15, 33, 39–43, 51, 56, 68, 71–72, 77–78, 82, 86, 91, 94–95, 102, 106, 110, 116, 120
conducting gestures, 63
Copland, Aaron, 3
creativity, blocks to, 37

Deutsch, Daniel, 36, 43n4, 52
Dewey, John, 33, 43n3
digital media, 47, 48, 67–69, 89–91, 115–16
dynamics, techniques for, 9, 22–23, 64, 110

electronic music, 3, 24, 47, 67–69, 89–91, 115–16
enduring understandings, 3
essential questions, 3
etudes, 20–25
Evaluate and Refine, 4, 30, 40, 51, 52, 55, 57, 63, 64, 67, 68, 71, 72, 77, 79–82, 85, 86, 89, 91, 93, 95, 101–3, 105, 107, 109, 110, 115, 116, 119–21
expressive intent, 4, 77, 81, 85, 89, 93, 101, 105, 109, 115, 119

expressive potentials, 3, 42, 68

feedback: application of, 39, 55, 63, 67, 71, 77, 81, 85, 89, 93, 101, 105, 109, 115, 119; constructive, 3, 11, 39–42; receptivity to, 40–42
feelingful intention, 4, 10, 15–16, *17*, 19, 20, 25, 27–29, 36, 40–43, 47, 48, 52, 56, 64, 68, 72, 78, 82, 86, 90, 94, 102, 106, 110, 116, 120
film scoring, 81
form, techniques for, 23
fortuitous accidents, 10, 15, 25

graphic organizer, 3, 11, 28, 29
Great Big Enormous Turnip, The, 107
Groovy Music, 90, 116
guiding questions, 15, 28, 36–37, 42, 47, 52, 56, 64, 68, 72, 78, 82, 86, 90, 94, 102, 106, 110, 116, 120

harmony, 19, 21, 25

idea development, 4, 37
idea extension, 33, 37
idea generation, 10, 16, 25, 27, 33, 37, 39, 51, 55, 63, 67, 71, 77, 81, 85–86, 89, 93, 101, 105, 109, 115, 119
I Know An Old Lady Who Swallowed A Fly, 107
imagination, 15, 20, 27, 36–38, 48
Imagine, 3, 4, 9, 29, 36, 37, 39, 51, 52, 55, 56, 63, 64, 67, 68, 71, 72, 77, 78, 81, 82, 85, 86, 89, 90, 93, 94, 101, 102, 105, 106, 109, 110, 115, 116, 119, 121
inner hearing, 20
instability, 16, 19
instrumental works, 3, 10, 47, 48, 63–65, 85–88, 91, 109–13
instrumentation and orchestration, techniques for, 24
instruments, 9, 15, 18–21, 23–25, 36, 38, 48, 63–65, 71, 72, 81–82, 85–87, 94, 103, 106–7, 109–11, 116, 120
introductions, verbal, 15, 16, 37, 40

leitmotif, 47, 48, 105–7. *See also* Motif; motive
Lily, 68
listening, 4, 16, 20, 21, 33, 36–38, 40, 51, 56–57, 79, 82, 86, 90, 102, 107
Little Old Lady Who Wasn't Afraid of Anything, The, 107
lyrics, creation of, 10, 35, 51–52, 72, 77–79, *79*, 94–95, 101–3, 120

Max Found Two Sticks, 110
melody, creation of, 21–22, 33, 35, 36, 52, 56–57, 68–69, 72, 78, 82, 86, 95, 102–3, 106–7, 110, 120
Mitten, The, 97–99
Motif, 15, 47, 48, 81, 105–7, 116. *See also* leitmotif; motive
motion 16, 18–21, 28, 67, 102
motive, 21, 23, 33. *See also* leitmotif; Motif

music, elements of, 19, 21–25, *38*, 52, 56–57, 64, 68, 72, 78–79, 82, 86–88, 90, 94–96, 102–3, 106, 110–13, 116, 120–21
musical expressivity, 4, 15, 16, 18–20, 25, 27, *29*, 30, 34–36, 38, 40, 42, 43, 47, 52, 56, 64, 68, 72, 78, 82, 86, 90, 94, 102, 106, 110, 116, 120
MusicLab, 90, 116
music theater, 3, 47, 48, 71–73, 93–98, 119–23
music theory, 4, 20
M.U.S.T.S. use of, 16, 18–20, 25, 28, *29*, 36, 38, 86, 120
Musyc, 67

Napping House, The, 107
National Core Music Standards, 4–7, 47, 51, 55, 63, 67, 71, 77, 81, 85, 89, 93, 101, 105, 109, 115, 119
notation; need for, 25, 67, 74; types of, 20, 25, 27, 48, 51; working with, 27, 34, 51, 55, 63, 67, 71, 72, 77, 81, 85, 89, 93, 96, 101–3, 105, 109, 115, 119, 125–29

Orchestration. *See* instrumentation and orchestration, techniques for
Ostinato, 15, 21, 22, 30, 110

Peers: feedback from, 3, 39–42, 51, 55, 63, 67, 71, 77, 81, 85, 89, 91, 93, 101, 105, 109, 115, 119; works of, 3, 16, 39–42
Piaget, Jean, 35, 43n2
pitch, techniques for, 21
Pitch Painter, 68, 90, 116
Plan and Make, 11, 16, 30, 48, 51, 52, 55, 56, 63, 64, 67, 68, 71, 72, 77, 78, 79–82, 85, 86, 89–91, 93–95, 101–3, 105, 106, 109, 110, 115, 116, 119, 120
Presenting, 4, 39, 40, 42, 51, 52, 55, 57, 63, 64, 67, 71, 72, 77, 81, 82, 85, 86, 89, 91, 93, 96, 101, 103, 105, 106, 109, 115, 116, 119–21
principle pairs, 16, 28
puppets, 119–21

reflection, 11, 29, 39, 42, 52
release: of articulation, 25; and tension, 16, 19–20, 25, 28, 29, 36, 38, 86, 120
repetition: in music, 10, 18, 20, 68, 90; as a part of process, 21, 36, 52, 56, 57, 86, 91, 95, 110
revision, 42, 57, 107
rhythm, 15, *18*, 19, 21–23, 25, 34, 36, 37, 48, 68, 78, *79*, 101, 105, 109, 115, 119

silence, 16, 18–19, 116
Singing Fingers, 67
Sketch a Song, 67, 68
Sketchpages: introduction to, 3, 27; teaching with, 27–30, 37, 42, 47, 52, 86, 89, 90, 95, 96, 106, 110, 115, 116, 120; use of, 11, 34–36
songwriting, 34–36, 47–48, 51–53, 70–72, 77–79, 94–95, 101–3, 120. *See also* lyrics, creation of

sonic vocabulary, 21
sonify, 16, 18, 47, 55–57, 73–74, 82
sound, emotional impact, 4, 9–10, 15, 16, 20, 48, 51, 56, 64, 68, 72, 82, 86, 90, 102, 106, 110, 115–16, 120–21
sound effects, 72, 81, 82, 119, 121
Soundtrap, 90, 116
space, techniques for, 22
stability, 16, 19, 42
stasis, 16, 18–20, 28, 102
Stauffer, Sandra, 42, 43n5
student autonomy, 3–4, 11, 33
student ownership, 16, 33
Swift, Taylor, 3

task, compositional, 3, 19, 28, 33, 110
Taylor, James, 3
techniques, for: articulation, 25; canon, 25; dynamics, 22–23; form, 23; instrumentation, 24; orchestration, 24; pitch, 21; space, 22; texture, 24–25; time, 21–22
tempo, 19–22, 36
tension, 10, 16, 19–20, 25, 28, 29, 36, 38, 86, 120

texture, techniques of, 24–25
This Is the House That Drac Built, 107
Three Little Pigs, The, 119
Throw Your Tooth On The Roof: Tooth Traditions From Around The World, 121
timbre, 19, 24, 110, 116. *See also* tone color
time, techniques for, 21–22
Today Is Monday, 107
tone color, 19, 33, 85, 116. *See also* timbre
Tonepad, 90, 116
tools, 3, 11, 16, 20, 25, 27, 29, 38, 42, 43, 47, 51, 63, 82, 90, 101, 102, 106
Touch Sounds, 67, 68
Twelve Days of Christmas, The, 107

unity, 16, 18–19, 25, 28, *29*, 36, 38, 48, 86, 90, 102, 120

variety, 16, 18–19, 25, 28, *29*, 36, 38, 48, 86, 90, 102, 120

Whopper Cake, 107

About the Authors

Michele Kaschub is professor of music and director of Music Teacher Education in the School of Music. Her scholarly interests include children's composition, composition pedagogy, choral music education, curriculum design and assessment, and the professional development of teachers at all levels. She is coauthor of *Minds on Music: Composition for Creative and Critical Thinking* (2009) and *Experiencing Music Composition in Grades 3-5* (2016), coeditor of *Composing Our Future: Preparing Music Educators to Teach Composition* (2013), *Promising Practices in 21st Century Music Teacher Education* (2014), and *Experiencing Music Composition in Grades 6-8* (forthcoming). Dr. Kaschub has contributed chapters to several books and numerous articles to professional journals. She is the immediate past chair and academic editor of *Music Educators Journal* (a journal of the National Association for Music Education) and currently editing the *Oxford Handbook of Music Composition Pedagogy*. An active clinician and guest lecturer, she has presented papers and workshops at colleges and conferences in California, Colorado, Connecticut, Delaware, Florida, Georgia, Illinois, Kansas, Maine, Maryland, Massachusetts, Michigan, Minnesota, New Hampshire, New Jersey, New York, North Carolina, Oregon, Pennsylvania, Rhode Island, South Carolina, Tennessee, Texas, Utah, Vermont, and Virginia, as well as internationally in Canada, England, Ireland, and Germany.

Janice P. Smith is professor emeritus of music education at the Aaron Copland School of Music, Queens College, City University of New York. She taught courses in general music, foundations of music education, composition pedagogy, and music methods for elementary teachers. Dr. Smith previously had a thirty-year career as a general music specialist in the Maine public schools. Dr. Smith's writings have appeared in the *Music Educators Journal, General Music Today, Research Studies in Music Education,* and *Music Education Research International*. She has presented sessions at state, national, and international music education conferences. She is co-author with Michele Kaschub of *Minds on Music: Composition for Creative and Critical Thinking* (2009) and *Experiencing Music Composition in Grades 3-5* (2016) and *Experiencing Music Composition in Grades 6-8* (2023). She is coeditor, with Kaschub, of *Composing Our Future: Preparing Music Educators to Teach Composition* and *Promising Practices in 21st Century Music Teacher*.

www.ingramcontent.com/pod-product-compliance
Lightning Source LLC
Chambersburg PA
CBHW060254240426
43673CB00047B/1929